Praise for Lost   ____. The Life of a Juvenile Lifer by Marcos Gray

Those behind bars have faces and names. They are people worth caring about, and their lives have great worth. Angela Davis claims prisons are one of the most disconnected places from the lives of free persons, yet many do not know where to begin to know those in prison. Start with Marcos Gray's Lost Innocence. Lost Innocence tells the story of a man who finds redemption in the context of life in prison. In his autobiography, Marcos Gray reveals first-hand the realities of the black family that recent literary work such as Ta-Nehisi Coates addresses. Gray honestly weaves together the broken threads of fatherlessness, gang affiliation, poverty, and violence into a larger narrative of faith, accomplishment, endurance and the power of a mother's love. His outlook is remarkable and this shows throughout his narrative. Marcos' story is not for the faint of heart. It is a story "written in blood." His story is for readers who desire to deal with the horrific realities of white America, the social neglect of black families, and the complexity that is human life. Gray's incisive writing is powerful, and his story is at once an occasion for empathy and a call to action. High praise for Marcos' vulnerable, honest, and inspiring work!

~Rev. Michelle A. Clifton-Soderstrom,
Professor of Theology & Ethics,
North Park Theological Seminary

Why are our prisons so full of young African American men? Marco Gray's story suggests one poignant answer to this haunting question. Gray's powerful and heart-wrenching autobiography is an account of a son who felt unloved by his father. He shares his story in a manner that is so engrossing that it leaves the reader feeling as though you are sitting in a cell with him. As you journey with Gray through life behind bars, you too will feel his pain of rejection, frustration and torment of his wounded soul. It is so unfortunate that his torment and self-hatred leaked from his own soul onto society around him, causing him to enter the legal system and the concrete walls of prison which he refers to as a "cemented coffin."

~ Rev. Dr. Alexander Gee, Jr.,
Pastor of Fountain of Life Covenant Church

Dedicated to my mom.

The only love to have covered me even when I was unlovable.

Lost Innocence: The Life of a Juvenile Lifer

by

MARCOS GRAY

Lost Innocence: The Life of a Juvenile Lifer

Copyright © 2018

Published by
MIDNIGHT EXPRESS BOOKS
POBox 69
Berryville AR 72616
Email: MEBooks1@yahoo.com

LOST INNOCENCE: THE LIFE OF A JUVENILE LIFER

By: Marcos Gray

Contents

Introduction

"I assure you that it's incorrect to assume that because I'm invisible and live in a hole, that I am dead. I'm neither dead nor in a state of suspended animation: call me Jack the Bear, for I am in a state of hibernation." Ralph Ellison-The Invisible Man.

The question I had always been forced to ask myself was, "how did I go from the youngest boy of five sisters and four brothers; the pride and joy of my mother; into a gangbanging, drug dealing 16 year old sentenced to life without parole?" I've long tried to answer that, but no one answer will suffice. The beginning of my life in the Chicago streets were plagued by devastating distractions: gangs, drugs, murder and prison all seemed as natural as the air we breathed. Genocide was so prevalent that it was seen, as acceptable; not only by our community, but society as well. This clearly affected the way in which I would come to view the world; the way in which I would believe life should be lived. The psychological paradigm had shifted at about 13 yrs. old, leaving me going through the motions of a "good" kid, but the facade would eventually be removed.

Since then, there had never been, a time in which I didn't consider my life as being comparable to a plume of ash that would expand and eventually enshroud Pompeii after the eruption of Mt. Vesuvius. This essentially meant that my life without parole sentence could be deemed the lava that preceded it; burning away every hope (though hope seldom was present). I suppose that from a distance it was interesting to look at, but up close and personal it was nothing short of catastrophic. This seemed to have been the basis of my existence since birth. Even prior to infecting the world with my birth, my environment was exposing me to a vortex of violence; a vortex of depravity; a vortex of death that I (and countless others) would fall victim to. It was much like the way the Bermuda Triangle devours ships and planes foolish (or brazen) enough to be in its geography.

The hardest thing for me to admit was that instead of screaming "mayday" like the Captain's or Pilot's did, I eagerly immersed myself into it.

It seemed that the easiest thing in my 'Hood to do was join a gang? apart from someone willing to give you drugs to sell, or maybe an unnamed bullet aimed at our future, gang membership was easy. I was, however, oblivious of the perils in the streets: rival gangs (sometime your own) shooting at you; police trying to arrest you- or worse, turn you into a snitch, and they were not adverse to framing you for a crime you didn't commit; robbers trying to fulfill their calling, just to name a few. Though I had been able to resist the longing whispers of the streets, with its alluring criminality, solely for my mother, but the shift had already taken place and it was comparable to the ones that occur on the ocean's floor when their tectonic plates cause a violent undercurrent of change without any obvious reason. I would find my life to be just as devastating as the tectonic plates that shift; creating Tsunami's on coastal regions destroying everything in its path before it turns on itself and dissipates. I had never imagined that the death I longed for, the death that I worked towards would have come in the form of a "cemented coffin", or what society calls a prison cell.

I could posit this was the case because I didn't have the luxury of thinking like other children, where the average kid never pondered death, it seemed that since death was ever present in my 'hood; 'it served me better (so I thought) to dwell on it because it would prove to be the thread woven into the fabric of my very existence. Thus, the magnitude of my erroneous Ideals seemingly had to culminate with my imprisonment, since death had eluded me. And though I thought that my life had only started once I delved into the streets, it was actually only beginning to end. I had always gone with a premise that I'd be murdered before 17 (wishful thinking), but an unimaginable benefit would reveal itself at the outset of incarceration: I would find God in "hell." While imprisoned on an unjust conviction, I knew peace would be an impossibility; its very existence is negated by incarceration, but God would still transform me into an individual who would no longer be "blood thirsty" but in one with whom He could be proud of. I don't posit I'm perfect; if I were I would no longer be human, but I am transformed. Though it's incomplete, it is genuine. Here is my story; at least part of it.

Chapter 1: My Mother's Son

There was nothing extraordinary about my birth on November 13, 1976. Our house was already full of mouths to feed. I always felt that they could have done without one more. We lived in a three bedroom house, though not small per se, it was quaint. Yet, all of its quaintness was negated by the number of people that inhabited it. Because of the volume of people, this meant that rooms like the attic and the basement were converted into "bedrooms." I shared the basement with two of my older brothers: Kenneth was about five years my senior and Steven about three. Kenneth would be off to college in a couples years and Steven was seldom home anyway, so it was virtually like I had the room to myself. This would eventually be advantageous, since I was able to sneak guns, drugs, and girls in without consequence.

I always felt that my life was worsened due to the severe asthmatic condition I was afflicted with since birth. I always hated that my lungs weren't just a little weaker; this would've spared me and my family the eventual heartache that I would cause. I also would not be truthful if I didn't concede that as being selfish, but that selfishness is predicated upon the fact that my psychological torment is worse than any physical pain that I have ever endured (being shot included). Though I was a peaceful child, I did hit my mom in the mouth with a fingernail bottle, permanently chipping her tooth. She told me that I was about 2 years old, so it wasn't intentional, but maybe this was merely a precursor to the violence that I would grow to live by.

There was already a strain in their marriage when I came; his antagonism towards me didn't help. His issue was that, according to his logic, I was too dark to be his son. I surmise that his unfaithfulness was causing him to be paranoid regarding my mother's. It's sad that upon my birth I never had a chance to be loved by him merely because he was ignorant to genetics; complexion isn't indicative of faithfulness. I hate that his disdain for me negated the opportunity for me to at least disappoint him, and not merely be loathed by him instinctively.

I can never forget what I deemed my first "love". Talisa Mitchell had been in my kindergarten class, so I was familiar with her long before I even had an interest in girls. It seemed that throughout most of my grammar school days she way the object of my affections, even if I had another girlfriend. This love started when I was about 11 or 12 and she was the only thing that I craved more than playing with my G.I. Joe action figures. She was by far the prettiest girl to have stepped foot through Marcus Garvey Elementary School. She was caramel complected, with dimples that seemed to go into an abyss and this only enhanced an already flawless smile. In addition to such physical beauty, she was extremely smart and would eventually become our graduating 8th grade class valedictorian.

And at the end of that graduation ceremony, she had awarded me with a kiss on the cheek, which I felt was more of an accomplishment than graduating. On many instances, throughout my grade school years, our teacher(s) caught me staring in her direction, and so to embarrass me, they'd call me to the chalk board to solve an equation that they knew I wasn't paying attention to because I was - watching Talisa. Though I answered the questions and math problems wrong on many occasions, I didn't regret my decision, how could I? I made my choice and it seemed easy.

Talisa used to hang with my sister Sylvia, so she was around often. She was in my class almost every other year throughout grammar school. Finally, one year (I suspect from pity) she decided that we should be boyfriend and girlfriend. This was done by her sending me a note in class that said, "Will you be my boyfriend? circle yes or no", this was proper Garvey "dating" protocol and I PROMPTLY circled yes. As happy as I was, I would be just as distraught in a few weeks when she would break up with me. I would eventually learn that she felt that I didn't spend enough (or any) time with her and that I was too timid (I was).

I can't say that it happened without warning because one of my friends, Denekia, had told me that Talisa was going to break up with me. But I disregarded that because I felt I hadn't done anything wrong; I hadn't done anything at all. I was a typical kid who liked riding my bike more than I cared about trying to learn the intricacies of cultivating a relationship. Though I knew that I wanted her, I had no

2

idea what was entailed in keeping her. I had an aversion to public displays of affections, but this was what was expected. And this would also be my undoing. At Garvey, the more mushy you were for everyone to see meant how much you cared about your girlfriend (I would find this to be true in high school also). I hated that I didn't listen to Denekia, but I know now what I didn't know then: childhood is nothing if not a learning experience.

Though I didn't satisfy her requirements as a boyfriend, I was quite familiar with the "birds and bees". About a year (maybe) prior to this failed relationship, one of my neighbors, April*, taught me. She was about a year older than I and we used to play hide-and-seek with other kids. This was the perfect way to waste summer days, which seemed to end too swiftly. On a particular day she took me to a neighbor's garage; all the while I was thinking just about hide-and-seek. She placed me beside the car and told me boyfriends and girlfriends use their tongues to kiss. The fact that we were a couple shocked me, but not as much as what I initially deemed gross about her tongue in my mouth. This was much different than pecks on the cheek that family and my sister's friends gave me.

It would become a habit of hers that whenever we played hide- and-seek, she'd take me somewhere to further educate me on sexual conduct. Though I would soon stop considering tongue kissing as gross, I almost found it linked to the smell of gasoline that permeated the garage that she preferred. I often wondered who had taught such a young girl that. There was always speculation that she had been mol-ested by family members, but at the time I didn't want to believe that someone would do that to a loved one; life would teach me otherwise.

The moment that Talisa broke up with me is indelibly ingrained in my consciousness. It was a nice warm day that seemed to have birds singing and a rainbow sparkling, even though it hadn't rained. She and a friend of ours, Dawn, came over and I expected for it to be like every other time I had company: we'd play video games. She merely said, "Marcos, it's quits." Before I processed her words, they were walking away as if I was a murder victim and they were my killers.

* Name changed for protection

The sun was no longer shining, it seemed to have been eclipsed; the birds had transformed into vultures swarming over my head ready to devour my corpse; plus the rainbow seemed to have turned into glass and crashed down on me. Despite this heartbreak, she was still the standard to which all of my future girlfriends would be held.

Genesis

I guess I can't truly dissect my life without delving into my mother's. Arlene Keye had married my biological dad in 1963, though she had a one year old daughter already. My sister Denise was already in the army by the time I had real conscious memories, but i loved her just as much as I loved my other siblings. She'd always bring me army clothes (too big) for me and show me photos of her with her regiment. I briefly wanted to join the army as a kid, but what kid doesn't (or didn't), at some point? She seemed to be having fun, but mainly because it seemed to have been the catalyst for my love of guns. Though that would never leave, my army aspirations would.

I wasn't privy to all of the abuse that mom had endured from dad until later on. I would eventually learn that her happiness was short lived due to his insecurities and guilty conscience. I knew that after my mom's miscarriage she was happy to have a child, even if the father was riddled with "issues". His treatment of me always allowed for me to feel jealous of the fact that I wasn't the miscarried one. I often wondered was my psychological issues from him predicated on his treatment of me, or maybe you really can inherit a psychosis. I always hated him more for making mom's life harder than it needed to be than because of his treatment of me, which meant nothing in my view.

The abuse often caused her to take me to her hometown of Dayton, Ohio, and I'd be the only one she took. We'd visit her mom and sister. We were always received warmly, and this made me wonder why didn't mom simply take all of her kids and never return to Chicago. I also wondered why she didn't replicate Farrah Fawcett's character in the movie, *The Burning Bed*, in which she set her abusive husband's bed on fire as he slept. Some may view this as harsh for a child to want

4

for his father, but if this meant that my family would be spared, then I felt he was a worthy sacrifice to ensure our safety. Because though he was quite blatant regarding his disdain for me, but you must understand that none of my siblings were safe.

I'm grateful that God had been watching over my mom, even though things seemed to say otherwise. It seemed as if God spoke to my father and convinced him that he needed to leave our home. Though my two oldest brothers had some input on his decision. The only "monster" I had ever known was extricated from my life; there was no boogey man under the bed or in the closet that gave me more fear (or hatred) than the man that impregnated my mom. And now he was gone physically, but psychologically he's ever present.

I'm not really in a position to divulge the degree of abuse my father had to endure growing up in Jim Crow South, but I knew that he had. I guess psychological trauma one endures during childhood makes it easier for one to commit it on others as adults. Plus, I knew that his alcoholism didn't help matters any. I also know that his bondage to drink was not the cause of my enslavement to it, but it may have played a role. Or perhaps maybe I just enjoyed drinking myself to a state of numbness when I finally did start drinking.

My father had served honorably in the Armed Forces, so clearly he had some finer moments, but the pride and loyalty he showed this country didn't extend itself to our family.

Their marriage of roughly 20 years ended, thus forcing my mom to enter the work field; she had no choice with 8 children at home.

She was going to need to find a nice paying job: she didn't. This made the ground ripe for a couple of my brothers to involve themselves in the drug game. Though mom was dealt a very poor "hand", she played it as well as anyone could've. It was hard enough to raise us on her own without a cent from our father in child support, but soon 2 of my teenage sisters would become pregnant compounding an already dire situation. I asked my mom once how come she didn't take Eddie Sr. to court, but she said that the only thing that she wanted from him was for him to stay gone, I couldn't agree more.

Sometime in 1989 my mom met a man who I've always felt was my real dad: Oscar Pope. He too, sadly, was an alcoholic, but not the violent type as my father was. As far as I know, there was never any abuse towards mom, but had there been I'm positive that my brothers would have something to say about that. He was the only one with whom I share fond "father-son" memories; we'd go fishing; he'd offer to take me to baseball games, he just was an all around dad. Not to imply perfection, but he did have a genuine concern for me and that was something Eddie Sr. NEVER had. I am grateful of the memories I did have with my real dad Oscar.

Ha would come into the alley sometimes and play "Crate ball" with us. (Crate used in place of a basketball rim with bottom sawed out). His love for my mom was genuine and they stayed together for over 12 years, till 2002. I lost him to liver cancer due to his alcoholism of over 25 years.

Chapter 2: The End of Innocence

As grade school became a thing of the past in 1990, so was the innocence that my mom and dad (Oscar) enjoyed. There had been a time where they would try to bribe me just to go outside, but a time was coming that nothing would keep me in the house. Teens are a complex bunch, even the normal ones, but me, an insecure and timid guy growing into a jaded and indifferent, violent youth; this was something else. And as small of a thing as my 8th grade graduation was, I felt that it was a big deal because one of our classmates, Jamie Kent, had been arrested for murder even before our class was to graduate. He was sentenced to 35 years. He was 14 years old.

I had my pick of school's upon which to choose from, and some of them were very particular in the type of students that they'd take. I decided to go to Percy L. Julian High School because most of my grade school friends would attend there, plus I had an aversion to buses. I never would've known that I would be following Jamie's footsteps only 3 years later, but that reality always possible in our neighborhood.

I wished that was the only thing I would've disappointed my mother about, but she had FAR more life altering things to concern herself with in the near future. From the moment I began high school, I noticed how "adult" it was. My childish love for bike riding and playing "crate ball" had waned. I noticed that though my mother kept me in name brand clothes, they didn't have the same "flash" as the drug dealers' apparel: big gold chains, four fingered rings and $150.00 baseball caps. The ones who really excelled drove to school in their Chevy Impala's or Buicks; all of which were sitting on vogues, day-tons or hammers. It was like they conceded to merely being a drug dealer for the remainder of their lives (no matter how short). I suppose those feelings were based on every other day it seemed as if one of the students were sporting a "R.I.P" shirt for whoever had been lost to the streets. Oddly enough, even before I dived head first into the streets, I always felt death was imminent; it seemed to have loomed over my cradle.

My decision to just join a gang in my freshman year did somewhat amaze even me. I knew of the gangs functions since two of my brothers were Gangster Disciples. I was never pressured by them (as I seen some classmates by family), in fact it was the opposite from my brothers. Yet when two Black Disciples moved to the area from Englewood, I seemed to gravitate towards them, despite the fact that G.D.'s and B.D.'s were antagonistic with one another. They had the latest gear, an all around aura that attracted my young self. Plus they were about 4 years older than I, so I was easy to impress (it wouldn't be until deep within the gang that I would see the dark underbelly and not only the silver side to it).

Charlie and Pereese used to be over my house frequently because Pereese dated one of my sisters. It was during one of those times that I decided I'd join them. And shortly thereafter I was to be "blessed" in (initiated by accepting a 2 minute beating), and informed about the laws and codes of the gang. Though I'd eventually realize my involvement was more of a curse than a blessing. In fact, the easiest thing about the gang was the initial violence upon which I had to endure, which consisted of mostly gut shots, chest shots and a couple of mouth shots.

I had been growing less and less timid, but with that came a negative side effects; an indifference towards people, even family.

It grew to become somewhat sociopathic in its nature. Even still, my joining the gang didn't automatically relegate me to a violent person. I would get there on my own volition. That was a subtle transition, not just a swift, short leap.

Prior to my descent, however, I did have an after school job working at my neighbor's establishment. It was called Urban Ministries. I had to fold, package and carry boxes full of religious material so that it could be sent to various correctional facilities and schools. Plus it was only a couple of blocks from Julian, so it was perfect. It paid me $200.00 every two weeks, so it was a good paying job for a 14 year old. Yet, as with all good things, they don't last and within a couple of months I would be laid off.

One of my co-workers was trying to get his relative hired and a 14 year old kid was standing in the way. So, in my brilliant thinking, I figured the only way to make money was to invest in a trustworthy trade: the drug game.

It was close to this time that I had started drinking after school, but then it started to go from that to drinking during and before it. On some levels, considering that my father, step-father, uncle and brother were all alcoholics, I suppose I had to follow suit. The drinking, drug selling and dice games in the alley seemed to have brought me the familial bonds that I thought were missing.

One of my brother's (Steven) was not pleased to find out that I had gotten "hooked up" (joined a gang) and he let his displeasure be known one night. He showed up and came to our room that we had shared in the basement. He came in and slurred something to the effect that I was stupid and before I was able to speak, he picked me up and threw me about 3 or 4 feet on a bed. But considering I was less than 130 pounds didn't make it difficult since he was an avid weight lifter.

Lucky for me that by the time he could do any real damage, our mom had been down there because during "flight" I had knocked some things off of the dresser. Though my forehead was bleeding a little, I disregarded that and ran up into the kitchen to grab a butcher knife because at that moment, brother or not, I wanted him dead. It was almost with as much swiftness that I wanted him alive because though I grabbed it out of the kitchen drawer, after what seemed like an eternity (actually only about a minute), I put the knife away and left the house for a few moments. I doubt I would have actually used it even had I taken it downstairs, but a year from that date I surely would've used it. I knew my decision to join a gang hurt my entire family, my brother just showed it by violence. This is what we're expected to do in the streets.

I had long grown accustomed to stashing guns for my brothers, so I knew a little about them. On more than one occasion did I put their guns to my head figuring that life would be so much better without me. I felt that it would free me from all of the rejected feelings I endured from my biological dad and even alienation from some of my siblings. I always hated that I wasn't the child that my mom miscarried, but I couldn't get my mother's face out of my head in the moments of my suicidal ideations. It was the hurt that she would suffer that wouldn't allow me to go through with it.

The sad reality is that guns are so easily accessible in the streets, so the fragility of a child's mental state makes the high levels of gun violence almost guaranteed. Though school shootings are mass coverage now, but even when I was going to school, they were regular occurrences. Though I know that it was erroneous for my brothers to ask a 12-13 year old to hide or hold a gun, they were merely doing what the streets taught them to do: to survive.

Ties Like ...Blood

There were a few guys in my gang that I was close with, yet I would soon discover that some would turn out to be the least trustworthy. They showed it when we didn't sell "nation work" (the gang's drugs for which you sell but receive little or no pay).

I found gang membership exciting at first; I mean, how could I not? The hierarchy instilled in us that we were valued by them, but we still had to learn the gang literature; you know, the "Code of Silence" and never hanging with opposition. But as with all things, the rules were open for interpretation. I found it exciting that I "felt" wanted, even though I had no plans on not hanging with guys that they deemed opposition. I enjoyed, nevertheless, the feeling of their arms being wide open, but in those "opened arms" their hands were full of deadly and positively destructive consequences. But as with all deadly consequences, they did try to guide us in ways that would increase the odds of our survival on the streets. They told us to always be mindful of movement in the gangways; they told us to always be mindful of cars driving without their headlights on in order to make sure its occupants wouldn't succeed in sending bullets into our bodies sending us off to an eternal kiss good night. It was almost parental in its concerns.

They also placed us in dope houses to sell for them, but it wasn't all bad because we had guns, drugs, and alcohol to sate our urges. But it was an uncertainty with each knock on the door; we could never be sure if it was a drug addict trying to buy, or a home invader trying to steal what we were making, or if it was the police sent in to raid us. To compound all of that, the money we were paid was merely a pittance in comparison to what the gang received in terms of profit, it didn't matter how many several thousands of dollars we made them, we still only received $150.00 for our risks; it was all for the gangs benefit, so we didn't complain. Had I been conscious then, I would've protested the maltreatment, but I thought I "loved" being wanted. I don't know what I expected from joining them, but maybe I simply grew tired of being invisible; the gang offered me visibility, plus, the drugs were easy to sell, but the violence that flowed from gang life had to be learned and eventually something to be de-sensitized from. It wasn't hard to hate someone who looked like me since I hated my every breath; this allowed for me to eventually see an infraction where there were none.

Gang membership, with all of its perils tended to bring notoriety (or infamy) and I wanted it. But the obvious and common theme is that EVERYONE wants to feel important and I couldn't escape the thought that attaining importance and notoriety was through the amenities selling drugs provided.

One of the B.D.'s that I had grown closer to was "Chucky". We called him that because he had a resemblance to the chucky doll in the *"Child's Play"* movies. He and I knew each other from before our joining the gang, plus we hung around each other kind of often. After we had made those ties to the gang, we had then decided to buy some cocaine to sell. We decided to get it from a guy named "Tony" because we knew him from the hood, plus he would buy liquor for us since we were too young; 13 and 14 years old. It may seem wrong for a 20 year old to help children buy drinks, or even to sell them weight, but in the hood, the degree of affection one has is gauged by involving or supporting delinquency and criminality.

He had sold us the half ounce (street value $1000.00 if made into dime bags). He also showed us how to weigh it, cook it, bag and cut it. He gave us the drug game 101. "Chucky" and I thought he was doing us a favor, and in his defense he did ask us were we sure that we wanted to get involved in the game. We were sure that we were. We had no thoughts of the stick up men or the police, but we wouldn't have been real kids if we had thought that all the way through.

It seemed that no sooner than we had our work bagged up and ready to sell it, the police sped up and caught us with it then arresting us. We never got a chance to sell more than about 3 bags, before we were caught. We were just going back to the fire hydrant when they came, because we had taken a 20 minute break to warm up. We eventually found out that Tony had just left the hydrant serving and someone had called the police on him, but he was gone and we were just arriving again. We had been taught to never keep "Work" (drugs) on us, but before we were able to stash it again we were arrested.

This omen should've deterred our criminal intent, but it didn't. Our mom's had to pick us up from the police station, but all we thought about was now we had some street credibility since we didn't tell them where we got it from. They asked persistently. We told them that we had found it, but they didn't believe us.

Tony, as a reward for our silence, gave us about $300.00 worth of drugs to sell, which we in turn were going to have to use to re-invest in order to compensate for the drugs the police took. The attraction with drug dealing is that the drugs truly sells themselves; We just wait to collect the wealth. Or so we thought. Chucky and I would receive probation for that, but that didn't curtail our criminal ambitions. We had grown tired of kids our age driving to school, kids our age "shining" with flashy jewelry; we only wanted to shine as Well. We would eventually find out what all dealers would who had been in the game for an extended period of time: it's full of many perils we didn't consider; from robbers to dirty cops, all vying for a piece of the money you're trying to make.

It wasn't too long after our arrest that I had met my soon to be new "love." Roxanne and her family had just moved to our 'hood from the projects and she made it instantly obvious that she was interested in me; she'd grab my hands and place them on parts of her that only a gynecologist (or husband) should be able to touch. I had been with several girls since Talisa, some sexually, some not, but there still was a twinge of timidity left within me. I could never understand why so many girls wanted me; maybe they knew that I was broken and they wanted to fix me. I only knew that my dad didn't want me, so why should they?

She was about a year younger chronologically than I was, but sexually she was far more advanced. Her last boyfriend was about 21 years old, so I presume he had "educated" her. She had a beautiful light complexion; her eyes were light brown and shaped like she was of Asian descent. As pleased as I was with her external, it didn't negate the internal ugliness. As much as I believed she liked me, she still was indifferent. I had long suspected that she was seeing her last boyfriend still, but one day her brother confirmed it. He said, "Marcos, you a cool lil' guy, so don't tell her I told you, but she still seeing "Boo". This was a catalyst for me to never trust or care about another girl again. This wasn't the last lie I told myself.

I couldn't understand her betrayal because if there was ever anything that she wanted (and I could afford it), she got it. I do suppose that my staying at her house from 4:00 p.m. to past 11:00 p.m began to wear her tolerance down. I actually figured since Talisa claimed that I didn't spend enough time with her, then I wouldn't let Roxanne say the same. It was odd because even the folks were upset with me because I began to shun my "gang responsibilities" of, you know, just being a 15 year old gang banging drug dealer. I told them that I could sell my drugs from her house so it didn't matter that I wasn't on the blocks as much. Despite all of their ploys to remove me from her presence, I'd always find my way back to her. Even with my knowledge of her unfaithfulness, I didn't end it.

I simply became emotionally detached, which bothered me at first because my mentality had shifted so suddenly; I was 'psychotic' in a way. It went from "love" to disdain in seemingly no time. I did begin to have some respect for her after she told me that she was pregnant by him. We had grown even closer as friends; I'd stop by her house to see her mom and baby sister (about 5 yrs. old). I was over there so much I was like a piece of the furniture.

Anyone who may have had to live a life in the streets can easily attest to these facts: selling drugs leads to needing guns and guns inevitably breeds murder. It was sad that murder had shown itself so often, even to people who weren't in the streets. The latest victim was my brother Steven's friend "Squint". He used to be at our house often, but he wasn't heavily involved in the street life. He died playing with a .357 with a friend at 17 yrs. old, and though this death was an accident, it still felt like the several other murder victims with whom I was familiar. Ed, Vernon, Reuben and John were past boyfriends of two of my sisters and they all were murdered within 18 months of one another. The saddest of the three was that John died before he was able to see his daughter, my niece Tanae.

John's death may have been the most gruesome and tragic; he never saw the birth of his daughter. His killers tied him to a tree after they beat him to an inch of his life and then they set him on fire (allegedly he owed them some drug money). I hated that my niece never met her dad, but I took consolation in the fact she wouldn't be disappointed like me over mine, but such is life: we die out here.

Depart From Me...Son of Iniquity

One day I had come home to pick up some money for a drug deal that was to take place and my mom and some Pastor were in the living room waiting on me. I was stuck like a deer in some headlights on a dark road leading to nowhere. He said, "Son, let me tell you that God loves you."

I told them I'd be right back and I ran from the house like Freddie Krueger was chasing me (not before picking up the money I came for) and I told my guy Ron to drive off as fast as he could; he did, but I never told him why. I don't know what kind of demon possession I had to have been subjected to that would allow me to embarrass the person who loved me more than life itself. I told Ron we needed to go get drunk to get the "stench" of the Gospel off of me.

This was apparently the last straw because my mom decided that I would be leaving Chicago in the summer of 1991. People often mistakenly believe that sending someone away will make them a better person (this may work on rare occasions), but we can't escape who we are. I went to stay with one of my older sisters in Missouri. Kim and I used to have a strange relationship, but years seemed to have remedied that; I was still her baby brother and not many of my sisters could resist my adorability. The crux of our earlier issues came from her throwing a glass bottle at me when I was about 10 or 11, so after that mom kicked her out and she went to live on the west side with some of our cousins until deciding to go to Missouri to be near our biological dad. I hated that mom kicked her out immediately after that, but no one would get away with harming me especially since I was still wearing a halo in my mother's eyes.

A couple of years after she moved out west, she then decided to move to Missouri. She and I grew closer as I stayed down there with her. Maybe she felt that leaving Chicago would help me out as well. Plus, I did love playing with my nephews Stephan and Steven (ages 6 and 3) at the time. Their innocence did make me ponder on just where did mine go, and the more important question; where did all of the anger come from? It seemed to have come in such a time span, but I guess the violent propensity in me may have been natural. I spent most of my time up there doing the same things that I did in Chicago, shooting dice and trying to get drunk, though that was more difficult with almost everyone a relative. That was all due to my big sister was intent on looking out for her little brother.

And as much as I hated it then, I can appreciate it now.

My biological father only lived about a block away from Kim, and I wouldn't have minded staying there forever had he not been so close. On the bright side, he made no effort to come see me nor I him. I was cool with that arrangement, but one night he really showed what he felt about me. On a night I would need him the most, he wasn't there. I became ill one night with a severe asthma attack and he wouldn't let Kim see one of his four cars to take me to the hospital. She didn't want to risk taking her car because she didn't think that it would make it to the hospital because it was about 10 miles away.

He didn't have to speak what I knew that he felt; he showed it. Had it not been for one of my aunt's, I may have died that night. She had drove us to the hospital, but all the while I kept thinking why didn't I just die? I would eventually learn that the hour of death isn't for anyone to know. I also must admit that it wasn't just my death that I was thinking about: I thought about my father's death as well, mainly because I wanted to cause it.

After about a week from the hospital incident, and about two months of being down there, I was ready to leave. My close proximity to him was like a proverbial 'thorn' in my side, and I wanted to remove it. I did have a few of my relatives accepting of me, but this was based on the fact that they didn't really like him.

I guess there is much truth to the enemy of my enemy is really a friend.

It's strange that the several hours that it took to return home weren't the same as it was once I was leaving. I had a lot more ammunition for my hatred for my biological; I hate that he played any role in my conception. I also had a feeling that things would be different once I had returned, but they wouldn't be for the better: they'd be worst. My siblings asked how I liked it down there once I returned, so I simply lied and said I did enjoy it. I knew that they too suffered psychological trauma the same as I did because of the man who was partly responsible for our existence. So our inability to really display love didn't diminish the fact that we did love each other.

No sooner than I had returned from Missouri, and despite my mom's request for me to stay in the house on my first day back, I was compelled to go outside to see what it was that I had been missing. The sad reality is that as soon as I made it to 99th and Morgan street, I had heard that "Twin" had been killed about a week ago on the same hydrant that I had been arrested on months prior. It had seemed that it was something ominous about the hydrant, because we survived many attempted drive-by's while sitting on that hydrant.

We had known that Tony, Kevin, and his brother Kenneth ("Twin") were on the fire hydrant doing what the hydrant called for us to do on it: sell drugs. A car rode up and opened fire on them resulting in Twin's death. I had seen the affects of this on Tony, because he'd known him for 15 years or more, so clearly he was traumatized behind that. It can never be easy to have your best friend dying in your arms while trying to hold his brains in your hands in a vain effort at stopping the bleeding. I had grown tired of seeing or hearing about guys dying, but at that point he was by far the closest one to me to have died in Chicago's wretched streets.

The last shred of compassion that I had seemed to have been murdered right along with Twin. It bothered me even more because I didn't even have a chance to grieve at the funeral like the rest of his loved ones. He treated me like Tony did; he'd sell me weight of drugs at discounted prices, buy me alcohol. because I was too young, plus he'd take me over to the East side when I needed to "lay low" when the police were looking for me for various violent offenses.

What 15 year old didn't want to be treated like an adult by his peers?

Though most people only relegated his life as another statistic for the streets; another guy chalked up for the hood unable to see his five month old son grow beyond that, but to me he was another dead homie that I would miss forever (however short that was).

The streets had raised us as it had our predecessors, so we knew that the rules of the street entailed death for some and prison for others. The streets dictated this sad end to so many, but most were oblivious of that fact. I knew that it was either kill or die, so I opted for the former despite my hatred for life.

Tony surmised that Twin's murder was because of an altercation at a club over his baby's mother a few nights before. He didn't think it would get to this point because they never actually fought.

I guess they didn't need to because after his killer found out Twin's hang out spot, it was easy to orchestrate his murder. As senseless as it seems, it seems as good a reason to kill in the streets since we seem so adept at homicide (or genocide); sadly I would become adept at it as well.

Sadly, at this time in my life, genocide was merely relegated to what Hitler did to the Jewish people during World War II. I only felt that our street life was normal. It had been this act to have caused for me to buy my first gun: a semi-automatic 380 handgun for $250.00, but I wouldn't stop there. I made it something of a habit to try to build up an arsenal for myself, which would eventually be four handguns (2 Glocks and 2 380's) and 1 sawed off shotgun 12 gauge.

I knew that drug dealing had health risks, which is why I carried 2 guns giving me a false sense of protection, but I figured that the quickest route to success was via drugs, and even if I died, I would still be a "winner". I had to sever ties with "Chucky" because as much as I was cool with him, he'd want to go buy clothes as soon as we made a profit. While I'm trying to buy guns for our protection, he'd be buying the latest shoes and clothes. I figured since his mother spoiled him, he didn't need to excel in the drug game as badly as I did.

As with all of my other "progressions", my dependence on alcohol progressed as well. I had started off innocently enough on beer and an occasional bottle of Jack Daniels, but one day while Tony and I were in the dope house (place where drugs are sold from) he and I started doing shots of grain alcohol as the penalty for losing hands of 21 Blackjack. This would surprisingly become our drink of choice. The alcohol had another side effect that I would not have foreseen in a million years; I began mutilating myself.

The first time was somewhat of an accident; I was at Roxanne's house playing with a ridged knife and she dared me to cut myself. Before I even knew how much pressure I was putting on the knife, I was cut open on my hand. It took a couple of seconds for the blood to spill, I just found it odd looking at the pink flesh on a brown hand, but once it started it was a lot of blood. It wasn't as painful, because true to form I was drunk. This was the first time I cut myself, rather injuring myself, but it wasn't going to be the last.

I don't know why I decided to throw my fist through this guys car window, nor why I squeezed a bottle so hard that I crushed it in my hand causing for me to need 12 stitches and 8 stitches respectively. I guess the good thing behind that was that I didn't do it at the same time. I do know that that type of behavior wasn't unprecedented in our family; my brother Rodney had punched his own car window out a few years earlier. We had always assumed it was the PCP that he occasionally took. I know, on some levels, he did that out of frustration. It seemed like a release-like shooting at people. On my last self inflicted wound, I had made it home before I passed out hitting my head from the loss of too much blood.

It was an ugly, sobering sight to see my mom's face as she was told by the Doctor that one of these days that I was going to sever an artery and wouldn't be able to make it to the hospital in time, which would result in my death. He seemed to think that all of that was predicated on my drinking, and to be honest, he may have been right. I did grow tired of injuring myself because it left me in a compromising position;

incapable of swiftly pulling out my gun if I had needed to. Plus one of the older "folks" was telling me that if I was going to get drunk and cause bloodshed, don't let it be my own, I would listen to him from then on.

I did try to stop drinking sometime after that, but it wasn't for health reasons. Her name was Chantelle. She said that she did like me, but that I was just too crazy when I was drunk, so she couldn't trust a boyfriend like that. I didn't like the whole ultimatum that she was trying to lay before me, and I had let her know that in as aggressive a way as possible. I didn't touch her or anything. I just had some unsavory words for her for trying to make me choose. I reasoned that our relationship could be broken up, but I could count on my alcohol. ALWAYS.

I knew that the weight of my addiction was heavier than my 130 pound frame could carry, but I couldn't deprive myself of the only semblance of "peace" that I could attain; it came only by drinking. Sadly, it made me more destructive and hateful in the process. I seamlessly embraced those traits, but I did hate that it created instability in an already fragile psyche, but since the streets were unstable I fit right in. I had become unrecognizable to people who knew me the longest and cared about me the most. I rarely figured that to attain happiness was either through my death or my intoxication. This was because I felt that I was unworthy to achieve "happiness", so I stayed away from it like it was radioactive; its very mention sickened me. This was what life was...all 15 years of it.

I had already been working alternative blocks because we had burned up the fire hydrant on 99th and Morgan from which we sold dope from. It was during one of these "expansions of my horizons" that I would be subjected to a veritable rite of passage in my 'hood: being shot. We all grew up knowing that this was a probability, whether you were a gangbanger or not. I was with a couple of guys who didn't gangbang, but that never mattered. Since they were so harmless, the last thing I expected was to be a victim on that day. (I can look back now and see how often we targeted each other for no other reason than for how we looked; I looked like folks.)

The red Buick looked suspicious from the outset, so I watched it up until it turned the corner like it was leaving the block.

I guess my failure to keep an eye on it is the reason things transpired as they did. It was after I looked away that they opened fire with a shotgun. There were only 3 or 4 shots, but they seemed to resonate throughout the hood. And the fact that they were so close to us and no fatalities occurred; this was a blessing I suppose. I caught about 10 buckshots in the ankle, and reasoned that no one else was hit because they ran; I didn't. I didn't because I reasoned that I couldn't out run bullets, or even arrows for that matter. I also, on some levels wished that they would've succeeded in bringing about the end to a miserable existence.

I wasn't even aware of the buckshots until after the adrenaline from the gunshots subsided. I always wondered why didn't they get out of the car and shoot the idiot (me) still standing there looking at them with disdain. I can say that up until that moment, I had never wanted someone to die so badly except for Eddie Sr. I guess that the moment someone's blood gets spilled is the moment in which they develop an appetite for it themselves.

The "folks" were as upset as I was when they found out the reason for my being shot. Roxanne and some Conservative Vice Lord (C.V.L.) girls had gotten into an altercation a couple of days prior for who knew what, but the C.V.L. girls called their gang brothers and that debacle only ended in my being shot. Rather, it was a catalyst for something within me to grow more cruel towards people. I had felt it was a debacle because there were no deaths and what good is a drive by if there aren't any deaths?

We had been plotting on how to retaliate for my being shot, and I must admit that those 3-4 days seemed like an eternity. We decided that we were going to shoot up the C.V.L. girls house since they got me shot and simultaneously we were going to shoot up the park that those guys hang out at. If I need to emphasize, we only were going to shoot it up if we saw any of their kind out there. No sooner than we had our assignments, as we were leaving the session, 3-4 car loads of the same type of guys we were looking to shoot (V.L.'s) swooped down on us and opened fire. I don't have any rationale as to why on this occasion I chose to run, but Pereese yelled for me upon the first few shots; I guess he didn't want for his girlfriend's brother dying on his watch. He grabbed my arm and I followed willingly. He lead me to a neighbor's porch, and no sooner than we made it there one of the gunmen came near and with the chrome glistening from the 357 magnum; it's a wonder that either of us is alive.

We had come to find out that this latest affront to our gang was that one of the older C.V.L.s, Lorenzo, had just been released from the penitentiary and didn't like seeing "folks" like myself hanging and selling drugs on a block that he felt should only be reserved for his kind. It seemed funny to me that this grown man had tried to bully the younger "folks", but they wanted to be treated as adults when it suited them: so in love and especially in war, it's all fair. So many instances transpired in my life that I can say that it was nothing but the grace of God to spare me. I didn't know this then. I lived by the streets code: retaliation is a must.

We had gone back to the plans that we initially laid out: "Spider G" was going to go with me and a couple of the B.D.'s from one side of the house, so if anyone tried to escape, we'd be there waiting for them. The other "folks" were going to go to the park to get the guys, or at least their gang brothers that same night. Though there was more damage done by our retaliation than the initial altercation, I wasn't pleased that there wasn't a massive body count. And then to top it off, one of the "folks" had stolen some of the guns that we had used, which caused even more friction.

The difference between the B.D.s and the G.D.s are basically in their own minds. The Black Gangster Disciple Nation was created, as a lot of the other gangs were created for protection, yet somewhere along the way they started preying on their own communities. After King David Barksdale's death, there was some "friction" over who would rule, so 3 different individuals all went their separate ways. Larry Hoover was in control of the Gangster Disciples, Jerome Freeman was in control of the Black Disciples and "Booney Black" took what was to be known as the Black Gangsters. Though all of them were family, they still are quite often antagonistic to each other, unless there are some "People" (anyone riding under the 5 point star) around.

I was infuriated by the lack of casualties; there were a few victims, but that didn't assuage my anger. I told "Chucky" that never again would someone be able to say that they got the best of me, though we did spill more blood. I still vowed to never let any infraction (or perceived infraction) slide; it had to be avenged. Sadly, this was mostly the case, and I had even extended this vow to defending the gang. I obviously wasn't thinking about the harm I was causing my family, or often myself for the matter. I was merely expediting my ruin by my behavior.

In the hood oftentimes enemies become allies. After a few more weeks of the back and forth retaliation—cars, people, and houses shot up—Renzo and I had grown cool with one another. He approached me one day while I was on the "Deen", so my first response was to grab my gun. He said, "Lil' folks, lemme holla at you." He told me he admired my guts for a little guy, and that since he wasn't going to be able to stop me from coming over there , he may as well stop trying, my girlfriend and one of my gang brothers stayed over there, so short of my death, I wasn't going to stop. It wasn't that Wayne was so cool, it wasn't that Roxanne was so great, but I just didn't like the thought of giving in; I felt that my dad took too much from me so I wasn't going to let anyone else think that they had done the same. It was my turn to take...and I "took" respect.

His brother Herman, however, hated my guts and told me he didn't like me over there. The catalyst for him to change his mind was that one day he and Renzo went to Wayne's house so that Renzo could flirt with his sister (who happened to be only 13 years old). Herman came and stood about 3 feet in front of me while I was on the couch in the living room. He said that my black and blue "150" ($150.00 baseball cap) was disrespecting him (blue and black was the colors folks wore). I just looked at him without responding, and he grabbed me by the collar, but I still didn't flinch. This was so that my gun wouldn't fall to the ground and had he tried to take it I would have been bound, no, forced to shoot him.

I simply told him, "Whatever happens, happens and I could live with the consequences, or die from them and it didn't matter." Suffice it to say, this shocked him because his eyes widened and he let go of my collar. I didn't say this to shock anyone, this was merely how I felt. After they left the folks who had been in the room were telling me how

22

"crazy" I was. I felt that honesty shouldn't be equated with psychosis, but I also relished in their thoughts of me being crazy. I guess Herman realized that the most dangerous foe is one who didn't care whether he lived or died; it was clear that I didn't, so I clearly could care less about his life.

This had an impact that I didn't foresee; Herman told Renzo that I was crazy, so he began to like me. Our relationship became amicable, but I still was under a premise that I couldn't trust them. I've long known that it was the ones closest to you that would be capable of causing you the most harm; I would find this out. I did drink with him, but I drunk with everybody, but I still was conscious of their reputations as being untrustworthy. I guess keeping a gun on me gave me a false sense of security.

In one of our drinking sessions, we were shooting dice in their home with a couple of G.D.s from the other side of Halsted. Though G.D.s and B.D.s had a volatile relationship overall, I was cool with these two. Their home was like a motel, except we didn't have to pay for the usage of the rooms. Their mom passed and Left it to them. The oddest of events transpired as we were shooting dice: Renzo pulled out some powdered cocaine and begin snorting it. It was odd because he was so young (about 23) and it was powder, which we equated, to a "white man's drug" and not "crack" cocaine as many in our hood used. He told me he got hooked in prison and it helped the days go by faster. I lost respect for him behind that because I considered drug addiction to be something for older people.

He was trying to advise me on his ill conceived plan of quitting once released, but he failed without really trying. He too began to tell me that I would "make it in prison". But in hindsight "making it in prison" is an oxymoron; who'd call prison making it?

He'd talk about how lucrative the drug trade was in prison due to the corruption of the guards; he'd talk about how a guys own gang brothers would rape them as "punishment" for rule infractions;

I found his prison talk depressing. I actually told him (and several others) that I'd be murdered before I went to prison, but I never could have imagined that the "murder" I would fall victim to would be a life without parole sentence. Life has an odd way of bringing to you things you had no intention of ever meeting; I can't recall where I read it, but there was a phrase about "the best laid plans of mice and men" that seemed so apt in explaining, my life

Another one of the older guys with whom I hung around often was a G.D. named "Looney" and he was just as crazy as his name implied. He had just gotten out after serving 15 years straight for a murder charge; the fact that I was a 1 year old since he had last seen the streets was lost on me for whatever reason. He was visibly affected by prison and it would show in the oddest of moments. As we drove around selling dope and drinking, he'd be "shaky" by the gunshots, whereas everyone in the 'hood are more accustomed to shots being fired than not being fired. Another instance upon which his institutionalization manifested was when he and I were driving around and a dope-fiend started urinating behind a tree while we drove past.

Looney stopped the car with as much zeal as one would when trying to avoid hitting a deer. He then got out and started beating up the fiend. I pulled him off (after I had a few minutes worth of laughter) and I asked him why did he do that, his reply was, "that nigga disrespecting me." I couldn't reply to that...at all.

All throughout high school I had maintained passing grades; they went from excellent in freshman year to good in sophomore year to all right in my junior year. I begin to have too many distractions to really care about school; I had begun to not even care about life. I really only wanted to stay in school to prove my 8th grade teacher wrong when she claimed that "our 8th grade graduation was the only one most of you will get." Plus, the real purpose of school was simply to show off what our drug income bought, so 1 felt obligated to stay in school for those purposes.

However, prior to my 3rd or 4th period, I was making my way to Study Hall this particular day because I needed to take a nap from another long night of drinking. To be perfectly honest, I had been drinking that morning as well; the best way to cure a hangover was by drinking, or so I was told. As I made my trek to Study Hall, this female teacher grabbed me by the arm and told me that I had to put my coat in the locker (they wanted boys to keep their coats in lockers so as to minimize being able to hide a gun), I had a quarter length $450.00

down coat with fur around the collar, so I was in no rush to put it in a $10.00 locker with a $2.00 lock.

Though this 50 year old lady could've been my mother, I told her that if she didn't remove her hand from my arm I'd painfully break it. She looked stunned (in hindsight I over-reacted), but she complied. As I was dozing off in Study two police officers woke me and arrested me for threatening a teacher and being drunk on school grounds. I guess the only reason they really arrested me is because the school kept 4 officers there during school hours, even on quiet days. I guess this day must've been slow.

Being picked up from the police station by my mom had lost its "shock" value because she'd done it several times before, though it was usually for drugs or curfew. I had no guilt over what lead me to the police station, but was yet again forced to see the hurt in my mother's eyes. It seemed as if all of the hardships she dealt with meant nothing to me, but I was so hateful of my life that I disregarded the only life that mattered to me: moms.

This latest antic had gotten me suspended for the rest of my junior year, but I had all of the credits needed to make it to my senior year so I didn't care. I never knew that I wouldn't make it. This suspension simply meant more opportunities to indulge in depths of depravity and criminality. My mom often tried to talk to me, but I couldn't see a future, so why worry about a possibility of being in it? I spent all of my days selling drugs, gambling, drinking, and spending little time with whomever I considered my girlfriend. There seemed to have been less tension between the gangs, so this was a plus.

My mom tried everything from bribery to enrolling me into Job Corps; they taught vocational skills to children with whom the Chicago Public School system had little success. They turned me down, but I felt that since dad didn't even want me, why should they? My mom would ask me, "What are you trying to do with your life?" I would never answer, but I was thinking, "I'm trying to leave it." I felt that life was simply a "war" and I was an obvious casualty, except in this army, I didn't enlist: I was drafted. And since I was too cowardly to make my death physical, I continued down a path in which I hoped someone would do it for me. I tried to "crash" into my demise by being destructive.

Even though the gangs were more or less peaceful, this didn't negate my animosity with some of the folks. They stopped tolerating me because they claimed that I had become arrogant. I concede that I may have been, especially after losing hundreds of dollars in a dice game. I'd always tell them that the money I lost could be replaced in a few hours; it could've depending on my desire to sell dope, but that desire was waning. But I knew that the catalyst of the animosity stemmed from one of the folks' girlfriend would flirt with me, even while he was present. I figured that if we could be divided over a female, then clearly we were never really together as a gang. But that paled in comparison to that which happened next to make me REALLY see those guys for what they were.

Several of us were at Wayne's house getting drunk, and some were smoking weed. There was a slight difference regarding guests. Tammy was this 17 year old Caucasian with whom we had been entrusted to watch. We had done it before so I couldn't have foreseen it being a problem this time. She and her friend Mary were visiting from Minnesota because Mary was the girlfriend of Marty (one of the G.D.'s who had moved to our hood recently). Whenever those two came, Mary and Marty would leave and we'd be responsible for Tammy. I didn't mind because she wasn't nosey or a nuisance.

Tammy wasn't ugly; she epitomized what I thought about Caucasions, blue eyes and long blond hair. She was somewhat "tomboy- ish", but I suppose she could have been deemed cute. She was real cool, so I suppose that some of the guys took this the wrong way. About 30 minutes after Mary and Marty left, a couple of the guys began grabbing her a little more aggressively than I was comfortable with. They were pulling at her shirt and trying to grab at her pants buttons. I immediately thought of my sisters and then when her voice sounded too close to a cry, I couldn't sit idle. I felt that they were trying to "bully" her and I hate bullies.

I told them to stop grabbing on her. One of the guys immediately stopped, but the other one looked at me confused, as if I had betrayed him, but I suppose I had on some level. I then asked him had he ever known me to pull out a gun and not use it? He didn't answer, but he and I knew the answer because he had front row seats to my violence. I knew that he had access to guns also, but often times the best way to defeat a foe is to convince him confrontation with you would be too costly. He knew our altercation would've been fatal for someone; his death or mines didn't matter and he too knew this.

I told Tammy to come with me; she eagerly complied. I apologized for those guys' behavior, because for some reason, I felt that I was responsible. I told her their intoxication was to blame, but from an experienced alcoholic's view, I knew that the liquor only brought out what was already present; this explained why my suicidal ideations were the greatest during intoxication.

I didn't believe the excuse for them as I said it, so she probably didn't either. She was trying to hold the tears back as she hugged and thanked me, but she couldn't and with the deep blueness of her eyes the tears began to flow like rain, it resembled an ocean wave.

I begin to hate the folks more because of this sight, but then I begin to hate myself for even caring. The rest of the folks just sat there like this was the most natural thing in the world: to attempt to rape a Caucasian girl.

This had cemented my resolve to distance myself from them because their stupidity was going to get me locked up (I had no idea my own stupidity and inebriation would do it). After I took her to Marty's house and she told him what happened he was upset more than I was, this was because he'd known her longer. He wanted blood, but I told him that since nothing happened, then he should be cool. I guess there was something to being a "hero" , because Tammy wanted to hook up with me for a few months after that, but I actually enjoyed being a "villain" so I couldn't be reminded of my heroics. She and I drank together a few times, but I wasn't eager to date outside of my ethnicity. It wasn't from a bigoted standpoint, I wasn't trying to preserve the African American race, I just thought I knew I didn't like Caucasian girls sexually...This is the logic of a 16 year old.

Friend or Foe?

T.R. and I became cool under weird circumstances: I was still upset over the Tammy situation. I knew how to harbor grudges, so I was still mad at T.R. for flirting with "Squint's" 13 year old sister at his funeral, but my real issue was that he's about 18 years old. Or maybe I was simply mad because I had a massive crush on her.

At any rate, T.R. was the only one left with some dope to sell, besides a couple of the folks. Yet, I was sincere in not wanting to deal with them, so I told him to let me sell his so that my customers wouldn't go to the folks. I didn't expect to be out of work for long because I was waiting for a page from Tony. I only asked him because my disdain for him had sort of waned. He and Alicia had been together for a few years so I couldn't really be mad at him. He saw how quickly his drugs were gone and asked me did I want to work for him full time. I was reluctant because I enjoyed independence, but that still had limitations. I was still forced to wait on Tony's suppliers, but my connections were always well supplied. This compelled me to work for him.

Based on our work relationship, I began to hang out with him more frequently. I even told him at first that I didn't like him because of the whole Alicia situation. He found it funny and confided to me that he had actually thought I was crazy for wearing skull caps in the summer and dark shades at night as my favorite West Coast rappers did in their videos. I was amazed because for all of the disdain I had for him, a huge degree of loyalty was linking my psyche to him. Though Tony hated that I worked for him, he knew that I could take care of myself; as much as a 15 year old can take care of himself.

Tony had hated everybody from the other side, even though they had the same gang affiliations. He regarded them as either cowards or untrustworthy. I understood his point because T.R. had been robbed a couple of times and he knew who did it, but they still lived. Tony had been robbed once, but he caught up with the assailant and broke his bat on him; this is what revenge should look like. I even bought an axe in hopes of being able to penalize someone if they stole from me. I felt this third world country type of justice was acceptable. I thank God that the only person I ever chased escaped me (we all know it's hard to catch a drug addict).

I was able to impart some of my ideals to T.R., such as buying guns for the next idiot that robbed him. I felt pride molding a guy years my senior.

Some of his own gang brothers would try to take advantage of him because they didn't fear any reprisal, but I had long known that your own "family" could be your worst enemy. Tony always tried to re-emphasize how if I worked with someone who is always a potential victim, then the stick up men may figure that I'm just like my employer. He felt I was making a mistake dealing with T.R., but I told him I understood his reasoning, but he knew me well enough to know that I would ALWAYS payback those who may have gotten over on me.

It would only give me a reason to shoot someone, and I looked for those. Though no one ever tried to rob me, the neighborhood stick up man would get T.R. again. I had been at Wayne's house this certain morning, at about 9:30 a.m. drinking. Though Wayne wasn't suspended, he just didn't like school; he was only a sophomore. I was halfway through a case of 40 ounces (Olde English) because I didn't like drinking the Everclear until after 12:00 p.m. I was walking with my 4th or 5th 40 ounce in hand going to T.R.'s house, which was only a few feet from Wayne's. I saw that after T.R. had opened the door he was disheveled, and somber looking; this contrasted his usual self. He told me that Levar and Bull had pushed their way into his house and took about $6000.00 worth of drugs and money.

He saw the mechanics in my head turning, and he knew what had to happen in my mind: bloodshed. He told me don't do anything because he was going to handle it. I told him, "O.K., I won't do anything."

Levar and Bull were both well over 230 pounds and 6'2 and 6'3 respectively, so they tried to use that fact against anyone who wasn't aware of the fact that they too can bleed. It wasn't lost on me that everything seemed to always happen in such close vicinity to the last event, but this is how it goes sometime. Then it dawned on me that it happened like that because I was always in the midst of the chaos. I found it somewhat ironic that the block that I had been shot on was the block that Levar stayed on. He too would be shot on that block.

As mad as I was at those 2, I was equally mad at T.R. for continuing to allow for himself to be a victim. This the behavior that Tony was talking about, but that didn't matter because he had been under my "protection", based surely on the fact that I desired to protect people (and if it meant shooting people, so be it).It was easy to gain entrance into Levar's house: he called T.R. a few days later and had the audacity to try and buy some work from him.

T.R. was on his way to serve him, but I asked him to let me go in his place, so clearly he couldn't gauge my intentions; maybe he just didn't want to see them.

As I walked through the front door I was shocked by the homeliness of the dining room. I half expected to see his victim's heads hanging as trophies, and not a grandmother's domain. There was plastic over the couch and love seat, a big crucifix on the wall right next to 2 huge wooden utensils (a spoon and fork). I sat at one end of a long dining room table that had a basket of fruit (unsure if it was plastic) in the middle of it, I couldn't believe how audacious he was for not expecting reprisal for doing that to T.R.; then since he'd gotten away with it before, he figured "why not?" He was wrong to go under that premise because now I was a friend of T.R.

Levar was sitting across from me at the table and I reached in my waist after telling him what he had been waiting for was right there. POP, POP, POP, was the sound to have echoed through the house hitting him in the chest, but he was still able to grab me and place me in a bear hug because he was jacked up on cocaine. I let one more round off hitting him in the hand. I tried to keep firing, but the gun jammed—Glocks tended to do that if not properly cleaned. I now knew that if I ran from the house I would draw suspicion, so I simply walked casually to Wayne's house since they were only a block apart.

I did make it there safely and soundly, but it wouldn't last for too long.

I had always thought that I did that for T.R., and I did, but on some levels, I wanted Levar to, if he survived, have thought real hard was he willing to be ready for a conflict with me. I had one dealing with him prior to him robbing T.R.: he had sold me a gold watch, that he probably took from another dealer, but since I knew that this was what he did, I didn't care I always felt that I could handle much more serious adversaries, so he wasn't worth a second thought.

As I sat in Wayne's house continuing on the case of Olde English, the police bust through the door, guns drawn and noisy as hell. My first thought was which one of the "folks" told them that I was in the house; there was about 5 or 6 of them on Wayne's porch. And though I went through the back, at least one of them saw me and told on me. They threw me to the ground, cuffed me and confiscated the Glock, a 32 automatic, a shot gun and a 380 automatic. I was charged with a unlawful use of a weapon for the Glock, but since the other weapons weren't found on me and I didn't live there I wasn't charged with the other guns.

All the time during the police yelling at me, I had a smirk, and after they took me back to Levar's house, and through some breathing mask he pointed me out to them. They then took me to the police car and while I sat in the back seat for what seemed like an eternity, an officer opened the door and told me that he had died. He said that after he hit me in the chest with one of the full 40 ounce bottles of liquor that they took from Wayne's house. As ready as I was to kill Levar, I was not ready to go to jail for it, but jail was the furthest thing on my mind while I was pulling the trigger; I thought of payback.

All the while, there had been a nice sized crowd looking at my latest run in with the police, but most had already relegated me to insane long ago, so this type of commotion was to be expected. What bothered me the most was T.R.'s cousin T.Y. was present with the crowd. T.Y. had often been trying to tell me that I was going about life wrong, but he had no idea I just wanted life to be over.

T.Y.'s eyes seemed to have been the only eyes that had genuine concern in them. I did see pity from some of the other people, but that I didn't want. I suppose that there was a degree of narcissism that made me believe I had a right to behave violently, plus environmental factors, father issues and a self hatred stemming from the father issues. These factors didn't allow me to have sympathy for anyone in light of my circumstances and the psychology it created. The problem with that was I failed to consider the heartache I caused my mother, but I felt that she should've been used to it by then. I guess it's hard for any mother to concede to the fact that their once angelic and innocent child had morphed into a full-fledged demon.

As I sat in the police car after hearing Levar was dead, I wondered where and when did the transition go from me playing with G.I. Joe action figures to casually shooting someone 4 times, with every intention of killing him. I began trying to acclimate my mind to being incarcerated for a long time, yet I was also wondering which one of the folks "snitched". I briefly considered killing them all just to be certain that I got the right one. It hurt me because I was the first person geared up for retaliation if something was done to them, and this was the repayment I was to receive.

I was trying to recalculate the shooting to have ended in my not sitting in a police car being driven to the Juvenile Detention Center (J.D.C.). I did learn that Levar didn't die, and though I had never played the lottery, I felt as if I won it. I did know that this meant that I was in the midst of a potentially deadly conflict with Levar and Bull; they were not the type to "forgive", but I was not the type to care who I had angered, especially in light of what they did to T.R.

My mom was at home when I came from the J.D.C. (Audy Home), she had thanked Nicole and Stan (her boyfriend) for picking me up.

Mom had looked at me for a moment and then just asked, "What's wrong?"

I lied to her and told her that Levar was trying to rob me, and since about four of my siblings were in the living room with her, my brother Rodney added credence to my story. He had told her that this was what Levar did; he robbed people. He didn't know that he didn't try to rob me, but the fact that he was known for it gave mom a little consolation. Only a little. She told me that she would figure out what to do with me before I got myself killed, but I could never share with her, or any family, just how bad that I did want to die.

After I had gotten out of the shower, I saw Stan on his car hood outside of our house waiting for my sister. He was a high ranking member in the G.D.'s and my latest act brought more attention to just how wild I was; and he liked that. The more impressive the act of violence, the more "gangsta" an individual is believed to be, I epitomized "gangstaism". My sister had told Stan that she was going to go to work for my mom, so they wouldn't be able to go out, but Stan did go out. And I went with him.

He had taken me to one of his dope houses on 115th, but all the while

32

he was trying to recruit me for the G.D.'s. He had offered me about 4 ounces of cocaine (estimated street value $8000.00) and for me to be able to sell it in one of his dope houses. As tempted as I was, I had to decline, despite the fact that the most money that I could say was mine at one point was only a little over $1400.00. I knew, that for better or for worse, I had to stay true to what I had represented myself as: Black Disciple till the world blew up.

He didn't seem too upset, he said that he respected that, and then we just began drinking before he dropped me back off on "The Deen".

This shooting prompted my mother to call my oldest brother, Edward Jr., who had lived in Canada. He and I had always had a good relationship when I was growing up, he would always try to expose me to different points of view to life, and not the negative realities that I had to face on the South Side of Chicago. He had met a woman from Canada and they married and moved there. Though all of my brothers, on various occasions, offered me sage advice, I still eventually disregarded it. I thought that I knew it all. What 16 year old doesn't?

I had respected my brother because he was determined to accomplish his goals, and for all intents and purposes, he succeeded. I recall one instance where he was almost left homeless because his roommate had gotten married and had to move out. Since my brother couldn't afford to keep the apartment himself, my mom had told him that he could move back home if he wanted, but my mom wasn't prepared for him telling her that, "I'm gone make it on my own." As he did. That always struck me as respectable because he chose the more difficult route of *making* something happen.

It seemed that he was there faster than I would've given him credit, but I suppose that my mom told him how urgent it was.

He and his then fiancé had driven me to the lake front, for I have no idea why, but it was a serene setting. He had began to tell me how much potential I had and how much I'm hurting mom, but as much as I hated the pain I continued to cause her, I just wasn't ready to relinquish the life that I was living. He was telling me how Canada would be a good change of pace, but the same argument recited in different words wouldn't change my mind. I often wished that they would've just bound and gagged me and forced me on a plane, but that's after the fact knowledge.

He seemed upset that I opted not to leave with him and his fiancé but that is simply one of the residual effects of being hard headed: unwilling to listen to people who have your best interest at heart. Though there were always people speaking, my self hate was externalized causing for me to be self destructive.

Though my brother hated to see me stay, everyone else around the hood had been glad to see me coming. The reception I had received for shooting Levar was far beyond anything I could have imagined; honestly I thought of nothing but killing him, not any potential benefits (or detriments). It also elevated my insanity in people's eyes. Yet, I never could have imagined that there was liberation in psychopathy. I had found out that Levar had robbed several other dealers, so those guys let me know how glad I had made them by shooting him. Though I appreciated the money and dope they gave me, I couldn't understand why it took a 130 pound 16 year old to do it.

I had not only been given monetary awards for shooting him, but places I used to be restricted from were now accessible; they did so with arms wide open. I wasn't charged the normal fees for entering the gambling/whorehouses (nor was I charged for the whores).

I still kept trying to figure out why so many of those dudes allowed for themselves to be victims of those two. I guess to some people it's easier to make money than it is to defend yourself. Though I didn't respect their cowardice, I didn't mind benefitting from it.

If I would have known that this would have been granted to me for shooting him, I would have done it months before. It was easy to disregard someone else's life when you have only disdain for your own. I was only treated like a "king" for a few short months, but at the end of the day I was still only a kid trying to be a man (if we extracted the guns, bravado and jewelry). But since the adults praised my depravity, I HAD to dive further in it. It was sad that I hated life so much that I equated it with being a walking abortion because I never had a chance to live. Or maybe I just forfeited it? But on second thought, it wasn't much of a forfeiture when each inhalation felt like I was chewing on shards of glass and each time I swallowed, I was eviscerating my lungs and intestines, yet being told that I couldn't even wince at the pain.

Weirdly enough, as hated as Levar was, his partner in crime was just as hated as he was. I knew of some of the violence that Bull had because on one occasion, I would witness it. It was about three or four months prior to Levar being shot, and Bull had driven up and saw me and Renzo drinking on the porch of Renzo. He knew or at least had heard, of our propensity to rob drug dealers. He asked us did we want to come along because he knew where a guy kept his safe house (place to stash guns, drugs and or money).He also said that the security was supposed to be minor.

He claimed to have studied the targets habits, so he knew that some money was in there. All he kept saying was, "We about to get paid little homies." We found out that this wasn't to be.

Me and Renzo was visible from the peep hole, but Bull was ducking to the side, because a 6'3 over 230 pound guy would have made them be on edge if seen. Renzo gave the phrase, "Y'all got some work?" (drugs). As they tried to take the chain off, Bull kicked the door in and Renzo and I barged in. The guy on the door had suddenly drawn a gun and had it in Renzo's face, but I was right on top of him with my gun drawn, so he relented.

Renzo was understandably on edge, but I was able to get him to calm down after we tied both of the guys up. We had ransacked the tiny apartment looking for our payday, but all we found was about an ounce of cocaine and $600.00 in cash. Renzo and I had kept the money and the three guns those guys held, but Bull kept the dope. We had decided not to go anywhere else with Bull, because for all we knew, he found more, but just didn't tell us. But to be honest, I never should have went in the first place.

I knew that Bull was going to come with Levar when he came against me, but I could have cared less who he brought. Though both of those guys were in a gang, their respective gangs didn't really honor them because they would try to rob their own if they could' ve gotten away with it.

They didn't come as quickly as I had thought they were; it was that that had bothered me. The anticipation of a thing often is worse than the thing's arrival. Despite the area being naturally chaotic, it seemed peaceful around without those two variables. I mean we still had minor altercations between rival gangs, but, you knew what that was: those two guys were a perpetual monkey wrench in the machinery of the streets. They finally did appear as I was on Wayne's porch with a couple of guys drinking, clearly I forgot all about someone telling the police that I had shot Levar to begin with.

I saw Bull's maroon Cutlass approaching, but I had a couple guns near so I didn't care. But once it screeched to a halt, then my adrenaline spiked. In that hood, anytime a car screeches to a stop, it's usually followed by gun fire. They were about twelve feet away, but I had to run only about three feet to get my guns, but once I did, I didn't do what I wanted to. I aimed them at them, but I didn't fire. There were so many "what if's" floating around my head because I figured that this would have yielded return fire.

The reason I didn't fire wasn't because of any concern for my or their safety, but my then girlfriend Taniecka had been on her porch right next door to Wayne's, so I didn't want her or the other girls on her porch to get hit. So I ran with the other guys through the side of Wayne's house until I got in his backyard.

All the while I told myself that I had done right by not shooting those dudes while those girls and my guy Aaron's grandmother was also on her porch a few houses down. That pill was hard to swallow, but I never regretted it.

It wasn't long since I had seen Bull and Levar that I had decided to have target practice in Wayne's backyard; I did this to stay sharp in my gun-handling skills. I set up about 16 bottles and just began unloading the Glock and .380 so quickly that I surprised even myself with my adeptness at it. I had no idea that this would trigger what it did. Tony had sped over to the "Deen" and told me that he heard the shots and thought that I was shooting at Bull and Levar. Sadly, whenever people heard shots, they assumed that it was me; sadder still is they were usually right.

I didn't tell him what I actually was doing, so I let him believe that he was right; it didn't dawn on me that this would be the final stroke of the signature on Bull's death warrant. That incident sparked the consensus that those two had to be dealt with; permanently. I don't know why I found gunshots soothing like it was Bach or Beethoven and though this wasn't Beethoven's actual piece '*Wellington's Victory*' where actual muskets and canons are fired, it was close. I wished that it would have sounded like prison bars slamming and keys turning (maybe that would have spared me from a life sentence or the guilty verdict I would take to prom instead).

Stan and I had hung out often (outside of my sister's knowledge). Clearly, he didn't want his 23 yr. old girlfriend to find out his 35 year old self was hanging with her 16 year old brother. He really told me he wasn't willing to give up on me joining the G.D.'s. He and I were at the 103rd Wentworth liquor store during one of his recruitment attempts, but no sooner than we pulled in to park I saw that maroon Cutlass I had trained myself to look out for. Though I had a gun with me (when did I not) I was reluctant to go in because my right hand had eight stitches from punching through some guys window trying to get him. I also wasn't keen on shooting him in a crowded store. I still went in, but I saw Eric in the store with Bull. Eric was a V.L. "chief" whom I had sold dope for and bought my own from because of his bond to T.R. and even me pre-gangbanging days.

The reason I bought work from Eric was because, not only was his work more pure than the B.D.'s, but he gave me good prices as well. The fact that he had graduated with my sister Nicole and I used to play basketball on his rim with his neighbor when I was a kid may also have played a role. He had received a scholarship to play basketball in college, but once he was injured in his freshman year in college, he decided to sell dope; he excelled at it. He too had offered me money and drugs to join his gang, the Traveler Vice Lord (TVL.) gang. Again I had to decline, because despite my often antagonistic attitude towards the B.D.'s, I felt i joined it till death. Plus I found accepting money to join other gangs sort of whorish. So I figured that I would "B.D. to the N" as we used to say.

Eric had took me to the back of the liquor store and told me that Bull had flipped, so he was under control. I told him that if the G.D.'s couldn't control him, nobody could. But he assured me it was going to be "fine". I also told him that the G.D.'s had a "S.O.S" (smash or shoot on sight) for him because he had broken the arm of 1 of their

G.D. brothers, Marty. I had to calm Stan down with what Eric eventually told me;"After today, he wouldn't be anybody's problem."

I clearly knew what that meant, and it dawned on me that I had a role in it, but I didn't care at the time. I guess he just thought he could run to the other side and his deeds wouldn't catch up to him: he was wrong. He didn't fathom how influential I was with both sides of the gang cultures.

Stan dropped me off on "the Deen" and I told T.R. what was going on, but he told me that he already knew. It was odd because as we were talking, Eric drove past with Bull in the backseat and two more guys in the car with them. There was another car following and I knew that this would be the day that Bull paid for his crimes against the 'hood. Bull thought they were going to pick up some work, but this was a fatal mistake. Eric told me a few days later that after they went into the house someone shot him in the head and set the house on fire to try to cover it up. I felt this bullet was long overdue. I felt no guilt over my part in his death, but I failed to consider that my life would be the cause of my "death".

His death had major implications for the area because with half of the problem gone, it increased the odds of Levar vanishing; he did. I guess that after his side-kick died, he had no other choice. I felt something different with Bull's death because I was a "spark" that created the general consensus that his death date was long overdue. I did feel fake behind it because of the lie I told against him to hide my incessant need to shoot guns, even if at no one. I wouldn't have minded pulling the trigger on him, but being the cause of his death seemed dishonorable.

Tony and I had been in our usual intoxicated state when a few days later we decided to view Bull's body at the funeral home on 103rd at Gatlings. We didn't intend to burst out in laughter at the sight of his body, but it seemed so deflated. We were asked to leave because we were creating "an unwelcomed atmosphere"; little did they know that everywhere I went I felt this was what I created. I kept thinking how frail our lives are because at that moment in the funeral home, Bull wasn't tough at all. I guess when portions of your face are missing and your body is badly burned, how could you be?

The concentrated violence which emanated from my pores was a catalyst for his demise. It seemed that I didn't even need to commit it to to use it.

My days had progressed as usual (if one could consider it progressive)', I'd sell dope, drink and have sex with whomever I deemed my girlfriend at that time. But, the thing that I "lusted" after the most was conflict. This was probably why I took it upon myself to avenge any wrong done to the folks. You'd be surprised how easily I found my way into someone else's conflict. This one instance my friend, Emil and his brother Jerry, were in rival territory to visit some girls ; the argument could be made that it was their own fault what happened, but once girls are brought into any equation rationale is usually on vacation.

Emil had told us after he had gotten out of the hospital a few days after, he and Jerry were on the porch of the girls whom they had visited, but once they tried to get into their car to leave, some guy had opened fire on them. Jerry was hit in the chest and arm, but Emil wasn't going to leave his brother, so he had his brother's head in his lap and and the gunmen fired again and struck Emil and hit him in the shoulder. Emil said he shielded his brother but heard the gun click and seen that it was a revolver and it was empty. (This was why I NEVER used revolvers). He was teary eyed as he told us, but all the while I was fuming with the thought of retaliation: it was a must. This bothered me even more than Levar and Bull robbing T.R. because I could've lost two close friends.

Best Served Cold

Emil was released from the hospital about a couple of days of being shot, but he wanted for his arm to get a little better for our mission. We had been plotting for days on how we were going to get those guys back, though for all intents and purposes, we didn't know who they were. We were probably more blinded by revenge than we were at being calculating, but we were able to score a few more points for the neighborhood after our retaliation. The image which had really hurt me was the visit to the hospital to see Jerry since he would be there for awhile; he was nothing like his energetic and lively self. He had looked beaten.

I suppose staring down the barrel of a gun and hearing your would be killer pull the trigger, but out of bullets would alter one's psyche. I used that as encouragement. Emil and I drove to the block upon which their shooting took place and we noticed it was a nice crowd of oppositions relaxing as if they had no care in the world. We parked the car in the alley behind the house where the guys were congregating. We intended to shoot everything that breathed out there that night; we came real close to achieving that.

It was a nice summer night as far as the weather went, but the forecast for the opposition was a barrage of bullets. I had a new 9 millimeter Glock and another .380 automatic. (Couldn't reach Stan to use his AK-47 he'd shown me on one of my visits to his house). Emil had a 45 caliber and another Glock, so we had ample bullets. The scene was chaotic as we appeared from the gangway firing at the targets. Those who didn't initially fall, were hobbling along until they fell and roughly two of those seven or eight guys were able to continue running. We didn't chase then, but ran back to the car and sped off.

The price of war on the streets is costly and we often think we could afford its price; especially when it was with someone else's blood that we're paying with. We made it back to the hood, but we couldn't share our excitement with those guys because I still didn't find out who told the police I had been hiding after shooting Levar. We simply changed clothes and this aroused their suspicions, but we played dumb. I had no idea that my descent into this abyss would catch up to me...far quicker than and in a way I NEVER could've imagined.

I had no sorrow for our targets because it was their fault that it had to be that way; they drew first blood, so we drew more blood. I knew that it was a real chance that the triggerman may not have been present, but one casualty is just as good as another. This lust for revenge was a strong motivation and often it felt that the elusive "happiness" only came in bloodshed. I knew that I was too far gone and that there was no turning back; I didn't want to. It never dawned on me that the people on the other side of those bullets were peoples son's, father's, maybe, people's brother. Yet, on many occasions I merely saw my father's face and not the actual target. That by itself justified my violence to assuage my patricidal inclinations.

Chapter 3: Appetite for Destruction

I won't say that there isn't some degree of "love" present in the gang culture, but I will say that it's inherently distorted. It's easy to see how like-minded individuals gravitate toward one another; toward people with whom they can identify. The only thing that I seemed to find more lovely was blood and alcohol. It was beginning to not only affect me mentally, but financially as well. I had began wasting about $100.00 a day on getting myself and the guys drunk, so this "forced" me to start robbing dope dealers from other areas to supplement my drug sells. I hated that drinking took me from a conscious state and placed me in a trance-like state. I also hated that I wasn't going shopping every two weeks like I had grown accustomed to over the last year or so; only to give the clothes to the folks or some girl.

I did try to help some of the other guys get easy money since I knew what it was like to struggle. Though my mom did more for me and my younger sister than for our older siblings, I still wanted more. I told the guys that they couldn't keep spending money as soon as they made it, but that they had to re-invest in dope at least several times before they started spending. They didn't listen to-me; the more I told them the less they listened. I brought myself up through determination and guidance (if you call teaching a 14 year old how to sell dope guidance) from older guys. The guys would rather whine than work, so I felt I should leave them alone since it was obvious that they didn't really want to work. I was only a year older than them so they wouldn't receive any excuse for being childish.

This in turn had some of the B.Ds telling our "chief" (guys with rank) that I was selling drugs with opposition; this was forbidden in our gang. I would later learn the reason for this betrayal, but it didn't make it any easier. They claimed that I had been growing egotistical. How they justified "snitching" was beyond me. I was only making about $400 to $500 a week from drug sales, so I wasn't doing much. Plus about $100 of that went to supporting our alcoholism. This was my justification for not just selling drugs but also robbing drug dealers.

Yet this money wasn't dependable. They wouldn't listen as I tried to tell them that if we want something to happen, we had to make it happen. Though I was doing "O.K." for a kid, I would eventually battle with a conscience that I had thought was long gone: I allowed one of my friend's sister to do a "favor" for me for drugs, so that bothered me, yet I found nothing wrong dealing with death on a daily basis.

Though the B.D.S. didn't like that I was working with others, I wasn't going to stop. I felt that whatever consequence I'd have to face, so be it. I wouldn't sever ties with guys I trusted.

There was this one instance which almost brought things into a full confrontation between the "folks". My gang brother "Bootsy" and I were arguing, and since I was drunk, I was probably to blame.

He had said somewhere in the argument, "You ain't what everybody think, you ain't gone shoot me." As right as he was about me not being what everybody thought about me, he was wrong about my not shooting him.

No sooner had he finished that sentence, I had drew my pistol and fired at his head. I missed him by inches because my intoxication had compromised my coordination. Or God was looking out for him and one of the guys had grabbed my arm before I could fire again.

Since we were about 5 feet apart, I guess things didn't end badly.

That could've been a potential senseless murder, but life seems to have less value in Chicago, or at least in urban communities.

Our deaths seem acceptable; I told you, we die out here.

"Bootsy" was alright, but understandably angry with me. I don't know how I was so unstable as to have allowed such non-consequential words to have enraged me, but in all honesty, I was already and always enraged. I was applauded more for my being a reactionary, as opposed to a contemplative person. However, in my mind, after he said that I wouldn't shoot him, my hands were tied; I had to shoot him. This didn't go over too well with most of the "folks" over there that night and they plotted jumping me.

Emil had got wind of the plot and somewhat tricked me into the car.

He told me we were going back to the liquor store. As we were driving for a moment, I made him stop the car and I went back to the block after he told me of their alleged plot. I had one gun with me and 2 more at T.R.'s house so I wished that they would've given me a reason to shoot them. Emil then drove to my house and brought my older sister, Nicole, so that she would calm me down.

She alone could do that.

Nicole had reached the block in what seemed like a millisecond, but I suppose inebriation played a role on my concepts of time. I don't know what exactly it was in our relationship, but for some odd reason I gave her words equal, or maybe even more, credence than my mom's. Though my actions didn't always show that. I had conceded to go home with her despite the fact that I had wanted to kill everybody out there that I normally would kill for. I hate that I didn't forget my drunken stupors, as most people claim to: I recall most of it.

It was interesting how calm it seemed on the block that all of this commotion took place one night before. I went and grabbed another pistol from T.R.'s house, though he told me to leave the situation alone, and I had every intention of doing so, but I would not be caught "snoozing". Some of the guys were still upset, but I didn't blame them, but I still was incredulous at the fact that they contemplated touching me, or at the very least touching me and not being shot behind it. I felt betrayed behind that, but I figured since Tony Montana (Scarface) killed his best friend, and Caeser was killed by his senator's and his best friend Brutus, then surely I didn't stand a chance of loyalty.

What else could I expect from young gang banging teens?

But I did expect something from them; to tolerate my violent and unstable behavior, especially when they didn't mind it when it was used for their benefit. It dawned on me that the ties that I thought we were bound by were not as tight as I had thought.

I did apologize to "Bootsy" because I was wrong, but I don't think he really forgave me as he said he did, but I couldn't blame him. Plus, though Talisa was nowhere on my conscious thoughts, I didn't want to be thought of her only as the guy who had killed her brother "Bootsy".

Taniacka

Taniacka and I had been seeing each other for about two months when the altercation with "Bootsy" unfolded. Yet, somewhere in there I had began to care for her deeply. At first my intentions were less than honorable, to put it mildly. I wanted for it to be only physical because I didn't want to go through any sort of hurt because of any girl; you can thank Talisa and Roxanne for that. Taniacka was about two years younger than I, but she had all of the proportions of a full grown woman. Even more so than the 18 and 19 year olds whom I had been with, thanks to potent weed and alcohol we'd supply them with.

She had been approached by one of the "folks" around there, but I unknowingly deterred that simply by my presence. He didn't want to sell dope, so I guess the choice was simplified for her. She lived next door to Wayne's house, and since I was over there often, it was a natural way for things to turn out. The first full day that I had spent with her occurred after about my talking to her for three or four days. After I got us something to eat, and me something to drink (she didn't drink) I took her to my guy's house, which was basically a spot we'd use to take girls to. After about 10 minutes of talking, we began kissing and I soon after tried to get her to have sex with me, but she wouldn't.

It's not that I've never been told no before, but never after it was so close to happening. This intrigued me, and it made me respect her more than I did the other girls; the ones who didn't know that "no" was in the dictionary. I liked a "floozy" as much as the next teen boy, but I definitely didn't respect them enough to call them a girlfriend. After we talked for about an hour, I took her home and once I sobered up the next day (briefly) and still wanted to see her, I knew that she was special. I couldn't believe that as calloused as I was, I was on the verge of being in love.

I didn't know at the time that she too would have emotional scars because of past abuse. I had heard her mother allude to her father abusing her, and this angered me to a point in where I wanted to kill him; this also drew me closer to her, even though she denied it. Though our abuse was different, its damage was pervasive in our

46

development as children. I, sadly, had always been some type of vigilante feeling that I had to protect everybody; all the while failing to protect myself from myself.

I also didn't know that she was the jealous type, and it was funny to me. I would intentionally flirt with other girls in her presence to evoke a reaction; without fail she'd cross her arm, pout and then storm off in a fit, but I found it cute. I'd allow her about five minutes and then I'd follow and try to assuage her anger. But as "cute" as I found it initially, it had become a nuisance within a few short months. I often asked myself why'd I put up with it, but when you have a 14 year old girl and a 16 year old boy, clearly the relationship wasn't going to be a picture of maturity despite the sexual interactions.

One day an associate of mine, Aaron* had noticed that I was dejected because Taniacka and I had been arguing, so he decided to take me with him over some girl's house over East. He was about 21 years old, but since I wasn't seen in the common light of being a kid, it didn't matter. He confessed while we were driving that he really didn't trust his Black Peace Stone brothers over there which was why he wanted me with him. It merely confirmed my knowledge that gang ties aren't what they used to be. No sooner than we got out there someone shot at us; the clanking of the bullets on the steel was aggravating. I always figured they shot at us because we were in a blue Malibu on Daytons with a custom made drop; it screamed folks because folks used blue as their color of choice.

The "brothers" use red. I knew that it was at a moment like this that Aaron would want (need) me with him because of my penchant for destruction; I fell into it with such ease it seemed fashionable.

They didn't even wait to see who was in the car, they just opened fire. In their defense, it was folk's car; Aaron and his cousin traded a couple of days prior. The sudden explosion of gunshots dampened my enjoying the intoxication. However, it did place vengeance at the forefront of my agenda and not the company of some new females. It was like the ricocheting of bullets had the effect of sobering one up quickly; once again I had been spared death, but I didn't think of it in those terms, but on missing out on death.

* Name changed for protection

I didn't know this then, but God stayed watching over me, despite me trying to find ways to shoot my way into a grave.

After we drove around the corner to see if we were hit, he told me, "I told you I can't trust these niggaz over here." I told him that I had the feelings of betrayal etched in my memory, but I knew how to make him feel better (I actually meant me). I wanted blood that same night. I wrapped my Glock (clearly my weapon of choice) inside of a plastic bag that my liquor had come in so that no shells would be left at the scene; I wrapped my t-shirt over my mouth and nose so that if anyone saw us they'd see only a skinny kid directing fury in the direction of his enemies (I had Aaron do the same with his shirt). As he was driving back around to the block I was half-way expecting for them to be gone and when they weren't I felt that God was rewarding me (in hindsight it may have been the devil).

We saw them still there and we turned so swiftly that the tires screeched; by then it was too late. Their attempt at escaping was three stooge-like because they were running into each other. I had been leaning over the door so recklessly that the risk of falling out was real had not Aaron pulled me back in when he did. It was like shooting practice because I felt nothing for them like a paper target whose sole purpose in life was to be shot by me. I found it odd that they were screaming at that moment, yet only minutes before they were probably joking at shooting some "scipes" (disrespectful term used to describe folks since we called ourselves "disciples"). I wanted to get out of the car to make sure none of the three that fell were playing possum, but one did escape. I told Aaron that he deprived me of my *Boys-n-the-Hood* moment when Ice Cube did the same.

We still went to the girl's house that we planned on, but didn't stay long because we discovered a slow leak from a bullet in our passenger rear tire. I was already paranoid because I had the bag of shell casings, which I was to eventually place in the garbage of one of the girl's neighbors. Aaron made a comment to the girls about this act, so this caused for me to tell him we needed to leave promptly. I didn't know if those girls felt sympathy for the guys shot; considering they had grown up in the same hood, it was a strong possibility. The hood one grows up in usually determines the level of affection for the neighborhood gang: and I wasn't from their hood.

I can truly say that this incident was the last thing I thought would happen when Aaron asked me to go with him that night. I still would've went, I just would've brought more ammunition. I never told Taniacka of my exploits, but they always found their way to her. It's not that she didn't know, but as much as was possible I kept her shielded from this mess that I called life. My regrets were not just how I was, but how come I didn't know why I became that way. I behaved without thoughts of others, and as I didn't want to do this to her, I did. Though I never hit her, but I used to tell her to stop acting like a kid; I wished that I would've acted like one.

There was one instance where she was on the side of her house and I was coming through the alley. It was past 10:00 p.m., so it was nice and dark. We were about 12 feet apart, and I called her and as she turned around I had a .380 to my head, but I subtlety moved it to behind my head and I fired. It appeared that I shot myself, which is what I was doing and I fell to further out my thespian skills to work. Despite the ring in my ear for about two days, I felt that this was funny. She was half way in tears before she reached me, but when she picked my head up they were full throttle. I felt guilty for that and even questioned why would I do something so cruel to someone I deeply cared for. Especially since she had known that I had long struggled with the thought of suicide.

I hated the feelings of guilt that I had long believed I was spared, but the more guilt I felt over that brought the realization that I cared about a girl. I had long decided to not grow overly attached, like with Roxanne or never again be timid, like I was with Talisa, but my attempts at remaining indifferent towards Taniacka was an exercise in futility. And I didn't like it the more time I spent with her, the more I cared for her. I couldn't even stay away if I wanted to because she stayed on "the Deen" and this is where I sold the majority of my dope from (this was also Roxanne's block and since those weren't the only girls on the block I had relations with, I was accused of trying to sleep with the whole block). That was an inadvertent occurrence; it was like murders in the hood; they just happen.

I hated myself (even more) because of the affections that I had for her, but that didn't stop me from taking our relationship for granted. In my defense, I took my own life for granted, so on some levels she didn't stand a chance. I was simply being what I had always been: troubled. Even after my fake suicide attempt, her words rang in my ears for months, "Why would you do that? What would happen if I lost you?" I couldn't have imagined that we'd soon find out. The words she spoke hit me, but the blows weren't enough to offset my psychopathy. Surely we "loved" each other with as much capability as we could as two young teens, but the damage our dad's inflicted upon us tainted every relationship we had whether we knew it or not. But her love for me meant more to me than my own family's because their love was an obligation; hers was optional.

I gauged people's love for me by their efforts to get me to do right. Granted, I didn't listen, but it was nice to know 1 was loved. She had consistently tried to get me to stop selling drugs; stop drinking so much; she basically was asking for me to stop existing. As much of an advocate as I was for my murder, I couldn't fathom an existence without alcohol. It had been very well accepted that I was a drunk because I'd start as soon as I arose and drank until I rested at night. It was like a birthmark; no matter how ugly it is sometimes, you simply have to deal with it; or have surgery. I never knew that my incarceration would be the "surgery" to excise it.

Whom Can You Trust?

All the time T.R. and I went about selling dope, but there was a lack of zeal for it as we once had; he'd been selling drugs even longer than I had. I justified it by saying, "If I didn't work, I didn't eat", but it was more like if I didn't work I didn't drink. We'd drive around neglecting clients solely to drink, shop and pick up any "easy" girls that we could. I mean as much as I cared about Taniacka, I wasn't a saint. This was our way to deal with the depression of three of our comrades recently locked up for robbery; this shook us because all of us would go and rob drug dealers from other hoods; and no, we weren't robbing from them to give to the poor; this was strictly for selfish purposes.

It hurt seeing guys that you grew up with trapped in cages (it hurt even more becoming one). We'd visit them occasionally while they waited to go to prison because they all plead out. They'd be ecstatic to see us, but the dejection would be more pronounced as the guards told us the visiting hour was over. That experience isn't easily forgotten; even if you're not an inmate, but they feel it the most. I always told guys that I'd never make it into a cell (maybe this was purely wishful thinking), but I strongly believed that my violence upon others would culminate with my murder. I had an ability to get T.R. to behave more brazen as well; though he was about five years my senior; it's safe to say I "corrupted" him in some ways. I had let him know that one Marcos on his side was better than ten of his own guys; I actually believed that, and so did he because he too was privy to the depths of violence I would commit when I deemed it mandatory. I deemed it mandatory a lot.

Unbeknownst to us, but the biggest mistake of our lives, well maybe the biggest mistake of T.R.s life, was for us allowing an old childhood acquaintance of his hang with us: "Bobby". He used to live around there, but moved to the Englewood area to sell dope and join another gang, meaning he "flipped." He prospered briefly, but then spent too much and go into debt and hide; this was why he returned.

I do understand what it feels like to believe you must enjoy life with things before you're murdered. This was my motto.

Bobby had been cool with T.R. before either of them started gangbanging, so this explained how he "slithered" his way into our midst. I personally didn't like him because I relegated him to a "pancake" (guy who changes gangs) because he had done so several times; this told me everything about him I needed to know. On a particular day, of no major importance, I went to T.R.'s house to express my agitation of his allowance of Bobby to hang with us, but then 1 seen the prettiest thing laying bare in his bed; it had a beautiful black surface; it looked smooth to the touch and 50.

The 50 was the number of shells she held in her extended clip. It was a Military Armament Corporation (MAC) 10 submachine gun that used 9 millimeter bullets. It was produced for the police and military (but they always find their way into our hood) capable of firing all of its shells in a second or second and a half. A typical cartridge held between 10-32 bullets.

After I finished salivating over "her", I recalled that I was telling him that Bobby couldn't be trusted, but he was not willing to listen; this would eventually cost him his life. But my loyalty to T.R. still had me spending money on motel rooms, liquor, and girls for and with Bobby, even though I didn't like him. After a couple of months of this continually, T.R. would see how detrimental this was to our drug dealing endeavors, I didn't care so much about the money, I just felt Bobby didn't deserve to be a beneficiary of my working in the street trade. I had known Bobby was one of those types to be around you, yet wish for you to fall; this bothered me because I already thought I was on the bottom of the pile.

Me and T.R. had shifted our focus on making money again, but Bobby didn't like it; he actually took it personal. I guess it was on some levels, but I could care less. Bobby came to T.R.'s house one day as I was on the porch (drunk as usual, as was Bobby), and I don't know exactly what he said to enrage me, but he must have said something. I guess in hindsight, he didn't have to say anything because I woke up angry simply because I woke up. And since I had animosity towards life; and since 1 was drunk, I don't know why I felt the need to interject myself in their conversation, but I did.

I can't recall why he and I had been arguing, but the underlying reason was that I didn't like him. But whatever triggered this altercation, it caused for T.R. to have to pull me off of him as I choked him on the roof of his car. T.R. took me to a girls house so that I could "cool off", and after more intoxicants and fornication, I was able to. The next day Bobby claimed to have no memory of the conflict, but I often remembered my drunken stupors, it just seemed as if I were incapable of stopping myself from indulging in the foolishness. Bobby had some rank with his gang and the fact that it didn't spill over into something worse was a shocker to me, but I always felt that I was ready for whatever so it wouldn't have made a difference. I had a vendetta against life, so I retaliated against it by pursuing death. This had always been the case.

I continued to be a nuisance to the Area 2 police department.

The depths of this was shared with me by Taniacka when she and her mother was picking up her brother from the police station and they recognized her as being my girlfriend. She told me that they said, "We gone get that little motherf#!*er" (this would be me). They also told her it would be before the summer ended. I found it funny that they were taking my life so personal; I felt that I was like a Clint Eastwood or Charles Bronson, only punishing those who deserved it.

I cleaned the streets up of its trash. I guess that since they were the ones cleaning up bodies from Chicago's streets they viewed it differently. And little did I know that I would be the trash to be taken out.

But as we were arguing and on the verge of a shootout, B.G.s Terrance and Mario were being driven up in that raggedy maroon 1973 Chevy Camaro that we had all knew to recognize. But before any shots were fired, a police car about four cars back, hit the sirens and begin to chase them away while a couple more dispersed the crowd before any bloodshed occurred. It seemed that with almost every instance of conflict I was involved in, it was never a result of something done to me. I always took it upon myself, like some type of ghetto "Superman" to try to "rescue" or avenge an associate. I can only surmise that prison would prove to ultimately be my "kryptonite".

Once I started hanging with Terrance, we'd do the same thing that T.R. and I did; drug sell in increments, drink in abundance, and sleep with any willing girls we could find (we found them often). I had hated selling dope so badly, but I felt that I "needed" to in order to furnish me with things I wanted (mainly alcohol and guns). I enjoyed chilling with Terrance because I had grown tired of the jealousy and backbiting some of the folks on the Deen had participated in.

I used to always tease Terrance about how long was he going to stay home this time for. He said, "I'ma stay out as long as I can." I knew that no one intentionally sought prison, but when our circumstances convince us that criminality is the only escape, so it's no more dangerous than inhaling oxygen and exhaling carbon dioxide: it's natural.

Terrance had the typical stereotypical prison build; about 190 pounds of muscle, tattooed tear under his right eye, tattoos of 103rd and Halsted with the six point Star of David all over his torso and the long permed hair as most of us did. He had been home for about a year from his second prison stint on an armed robbery charge after being gone for four years straight (that sounded like an eternity to me then). If we didn't have prison waiting for us, we knew that the streets released persistent screams of death howling from the concrete; bullets consistently took lives without asking permission, or if the bullets "felt" generous, it would only cause physical and emotional pains or paralyze you. The death in the air blew like an urn full of ashes in a tornado, all the while our lives were treated as the ashes in said wind.

Throughout this time some would try to tell me that I had a problem with alcohol, but I countered that my only, "problem" with it was when I ran out of it. I had evolved from beer to gin until I finally met the drink of my dreams: grain alcohol. This "evolvement" came accidently. Tony and I were selling in a dope house about two years prior and we ran out of alcohol; he didn't want to drive in the rain for fear that he'd miss customers, and I didn't want to drive in the rain because he didn't want me to drive his car in the rain since I was only about 14 years old. We saw what the fiends were using to ignite their "crack" with, and in our "genius" we thought it would be fun to force the loser of Blackjack 21 to drink shots of it; I was hooked, despite the fact it tasted like I was drinking gasoline.

The interesting thing about my decision to hang with Terrance was that I also called myself "laying low" from the police, but how low was I really lying only about 15 blocks in the opposite direction?

I guess, in hindsight, it was actually me trying to run from myself, which was an exercise in futility I just wanted to "escape", but I couldn't escape myself. I hung with Terrance for a total of about six weeks, but after growing tired of taking $20.00 girls to $10.00 motels, I grew tired of the monotony. Plus, despite how I felt about some of the folks on the Deen, I liked being over there because it seemed to be more of a chance I would have at getting shot to death. I looked forward to biting the fatal bullet that I knew was waiting for me; I would relish it. I don't imply that the other side was any safer, especially since we were products of our environments, so we produced violence in turn. A smarter person would assess my enjoyment for external conflict as being an indication of the internal conflict I had. They would be right.

Defining Moment

I don't posit that I had some type of prophetic capability, but this particular day the dark cloud that hovered over me seemed closer. Though the day started off as usual: awoke to hate the previous nights hangover, showered, made sure my pistols were loaded (they always were) and begin drinking beer until I made it to the liquor store.

This day progressed as usual, but since it was July 3, 1993, I figured I'd celebrate America's independence, even though I never felt I benefitted from it. So as I sat "celebrating" Independence Day Eve, I was oblivious at how much I was in bondage only to my drinking.

I guess we could conclude that I was an alcoholic (minus the meetings). I started drinking merely to emulate the older guys from the 'hood that I idolized. I found something cool about their barely being able to stand and slurring their words. I guess it would take years of living to realize how foolish they were then, but in my pre-teen and teen years, it was to be aspired to. It was about 10:00 p.m. and after an entire day of drinking (everyday was an entire day of drinking), Tony and Derrick, a friend of his, drove up. Though Tony and I didn't hang with each other much anymore, my loyalty to him wasn't gone. Since my liquor was running low, I invited myself with those two to go to the liquor store. And though I didn't know Derrick closely, he would try to convince me that I needed to stop drinking so heavily because everybody knew how foolishly I behaved when I was drunk.

Since I didn't know him, it was easy to disregard his advice. Derrick used to live around the hood, but his family moved to a nice suburb. He was in his junior year at college, so his hanging with Tony was somewhat odd, but the ties that bind us to one another can't be severed by education. Before I actually got in Derrick's car one of my B.D. brothers told Tony, "Don't jag my folks off" (slang for don't send me on a suicide/silly mission). It never dawned on me how prophetic Charlie was. Tony just smiled and we were on our way to re-fuel since we were low on alcohol. As we drank and listened to 2Pac's song *Definition of A Thug Nigga,* I digested every lyric from it, especially the opening ones: "*I play the cards I was giving, I thank God that I'm living...and I pack a nine until it's time to go to prison.*"

Even as the music blared, I thought I heard them talking about a crime, but it dawned on me that they actually were talking about a crime, but I could care less. I found this odd because the car they followed didn't "scream" drug dealer. I don't know how long we followed because I nodded a couple of times, so it could have been ten or thirty minutes. At any rate, the car that was being followed pulled into a seemingly huge two- car garage and it seemed that Tony was out of Derrick's car before he could hit the brakes. I instinctively got out after Tony, whether because I got in with him or maybe my inherent criminal mentality (as the state's attorney posited). And since I had long known that my "angelic" status had been revoked (even by mom's standards) I understood not receiving the "benefit of the doubt."

Tony had grabbed her driver door handle and told her to be quiet; from then on, she begin to scream, "No...Don't."

And since my inebriated state wouldn't allow for me to rationalize my environment, I stayed in the garage. I don't know what crossed her mind, but it was probably rape since she was a Caucasian and we were of African descent; this country had long posited that black men lived only to rape Caucasian women. But I do know what crossed my mind; "What the hell are you doing Marcos?" This was unlike any crime I had ever been a part of. I was used to shooting people for retaliation for any perceived infraction against those with whom I had loyalty to, but to attack civilians seemed...wrong. Tony had the wrist of her arm pulling her from the car, but not before she accidently popped the trunk as she attempted to lock the door.

After Tony ordered the keys from her, she threw them in the trunk as she was being lead from the seat of the car. He ordered her to get them, and after he pushed her in the trunk to get them she grabbed the gun; in his fear (or panic) he shot her once in the head. Violence never bothered me because of where we lived, but this area didn't seem like it should have to endure the violence our 'hood endured. I looked inside of the trunk to see if that really happened: it did. And it bothered me that my conscience chose such an inopportune time to resurface. I'd never surmise that Tony was right, but when a gun is aimed at your head, I'd think compliance would be warranted, and I don't think screaming and grabbing the gun would be wise. Granted, I may not be an authority on such behavior because the only gun ever held to my head was my own, I didn't know exactly how things would change, but I definitely felt that they would.

Derrick dropped us off at Tony's house, but we still didn't call it a night; Tony and I got into his car and drove to a local "Subway" restaurant to nourish ourselves. I suppose the fact that there were two policeman there eating should have been an indication to the "change" that was coming. We got our food and promptly left only to drive around in silence for about twenty minutes before he dropped me off at home. And the nauseous feeling I had suppressed for most of the night grew stronger.

I saw my brother, Steven, laying on the floor watching videos far drunker than I was, but I knew I couldn't talk to him about the nights events; though I wanted to badly. I knew he'd be mad at me for being stupid, plus I didn't wish to bring someone else into the errors I had made that night; hell, throughout my young life. I also felt he couldn't understand me; no one could.

That night I found myself doing something I had never done before: I prayed to God. As hostile as I was towards Him, I never doubted his existence. I just felt that he didn't care about people in my demographic; in his defense, people in my demographic didn't care about each other either. And in true "God" fashion, He allowed me to see the face of the dead woman in my dreams that night. It only then seemed to dawn on me of the irreversibility; of the finality of death, though I viewed my own death differently because my death was going to be an escape from a miserable existence. So instead of finding absolution from God, I found more guilt over the death and I hated that I cared.

But, this didn't imply that I sprouted wings and begin playing melodic tunes on harps, but it only increased my desire for intoxication because it was something else that I needed to forget; something else I needed to escape.

It would take decades into the future for me to really see how the nourishment of my alcoholic tendencies only malnourished my common sense, on August 20, 1993 I had been doing the usual: drinking myself into oblivion, which was probably the reason for my fighting a police officer whose mom stayed near. I can't say why we argued, but as he kept getting loud with me, it just seemed like a bright idea to hit him in his mouth, so I did. But as with most of my "bright ideas", they were masked by inebriation because at the end of the fight I would suffer a broken jaw; I wouldn't notice until an hour later.

The only reason I wasn't able to kill this officer was because T.R. wouldn't allow me access to my guns, which I had begun to keep in his yard so as to not replicate shooting at friends. He drug me to his car and drove me home and all the while I was in disbelief.

As I was dropped off, I decided to eat some chicken that had been cooked the night before, but I found it odd that my mouth didn't "work" like it was supposed to. My appetite seemed to have come from out of nowhere; there's nothing like being beaten to give you an appetite. I was still trying to figure out why I couldn't eat when the police knocked on the door and arrested me for assault on an officer and an unlawful use of a weapon (despite no gun being drawn). I ended up at the 111th police station that so diligently sought me, but I wasn't there long because my mom was present within 30 minutes. Before they let me go they told me, "See you soon," but my inebriated state was waning, and the pain was coming faster than I could process it, so their words meant nothing to me.

The look of pain over my mother's face haunted me; I immediately saw all of the mess her children had put her through: my brother's battle with leukemia; now Steven was a drunk; my brother, Rodney's battle with depression and drugs; two teenage daughters pregnant at the same time; and now a 16 year old alcoholic lunatic. It was as if the pain that I was in, she osmotically suffered because of the fact that I passed through her birth canal and it was still connected; yet I seemed to act as if it was only through genetics. As we sat in a hospital waiting room for 45 minutes I convinced her that we needed to go to another one, because as hurt as I was, I was more bothered by waiting in the pain like I didn't matter; though I would agree.

The wait was virtually non-existent, so it seemed that I had made a right decision for once. I was bothered by the look my mother had on her face; it was the *"what's wrong with you look"*, I had become an expert on deciphering it. I hated how I disregarded how precious her heart was, but not only did I not protect it, I seemed to "throw" rocks at it knowing that it was as priceless as any antique vase. I seemed to try to knock it from its perch even though I loved her from the depths of my heart; sadly I admit that my heart was shallow. I was no longer her little "angel", my halo had long since grew spikes around it, slipping down to my neck choking any goodness from me.

Reap The Whirlwind

They placed wires through my teeth to realign the fractures. I was given an anesthetic compound, but the pain was now much more pronounced because of the dissipation of my inebriation. They kept me in the hospital for two days for observation, in which those days consisted of changing the TV for entertainment. I found nothing of interest, and then I noticed a *Gideon's Bible* peeking out from a drawer.

I never could have foreseen that as being a life altering moment. I picked it up to try to read it, but it seemed Greek; the "thee's" and "thou's" gave me a headache, but I still decided to take it home.

Once I got home, I promptly placed the Bible in a drawer with some drugs and a gun. I also noticed that it was hard trying to drink alcohol with wires (thank God for straws). I went to the "Deen", but Taniacka quickly took me home saying I shouldn't be out like that. I had no idea this would be the last time we'd be together sexually, but maybe she did because she placed kisses on my cheeks so gentle that it felt like I was being tickled by a feather.

After I took her home, I had found out that Tony had been incarcerated for the July 3rd murder. My sister, Nicole, was adamant on me leaving to Minnesota with one of the folks who stayed down there that we knew. I told her not to worry because Tony wasn't going to snitch; I was right, he wouldn't. His mom would.

I can look back and see how my stubborn tendencies always put me in precarious positions. I was blinded by what I saw in the streets, but to be honest, I never expected to live long enough to endure jail. I convinced her that I could stay in Chicago because I had a penchant for making stupid decisions look fashionable. A couple of days later me, Nicole and T.R. were picked up by the police and taken for questioning. I played the injured, doe-eyed kid; "I don't know" had become my favorite catch-phrase. I guess they grew tired of trying to decipher what I was mumbling through the wires. Before they let us go, they asked me about Bull. Tony had told them Bull was with him, but the problem was that they discovered Bull had been dead for about 2-3 weeks. They fingerprinted us and released us and I felt guilty for having brought my sister into this, but they only questioned her because they knew she had a baby with Tony.

***

After being let go, I foolishly believed that this was the end of it. As if there would be no consequence for my foolishness, or for my presence at the scene of a tragic murder. The next day, two detectives appeared and told my mom that they wanted to speak with me again, but that her presence wasn't needed. I simply believed it was going to go as it did the day before, because had I known that over 20 years of being in a cemented coffin waited, I would have simply opted for the real one and came upstairs shooting, either to kill my would be arresting officers or have them do me the favor by putting me out of my misery. I found out while I was in the car being driven to the station that my prints matched some found at the crime scene.

This August 22, 1993 will forever be relegated to "D-Day" status, as if it was June 6, 1944 all over again. It will forever be infamous. I had always thought that a violent death would follow my violent life. I regretted not listening to my brothers as they attempted to tell me how to navigate the streets without prison or death; but their advice didn't seem like too much fun. And no sooner than we were arrested for this crime, the police began to inquire about a murder that occurred a couple of months before this one. I guess the adage "when it rains, it pours" couldn't be any more true.

It seemed as if my Harry Houdini impersonations were over with because there seemed to be no visible escape hatch in which to release myself.

I began to regret that I wasn't sent to the juvenile Illinois Department of Corrections for shooting Lemar, or at least for not being in enough altercations to have guaranteed my murder. After an extensive hour questioning while being denied my pain medication, I relented to their pressure and signed a statement (this would be the reason for a re-trial because interrogating a minor without his guardian or pain medication was deemed "unacceptable" by the Appellate Court).

I was allowed to see my mom and Oscar only briefly because after I signed the statement, they "miraculously" appeared (they were there all along). I was taken to the Juvenile Detention Center (Audy Home) and the pain from my jaw was almost negated by the psychological torture of what I was facing. The room was about 8x9 with a steel sink connected to the tiny toilet. There was a glass door to monitor the juveniles, but I was placed in the medical isolation unit due to the wired jaw I endured. They told me that the doors were see-through because juveniles were prone to commit suicide down there; little... did they know I was prone to do it prior to incarceration. After a night of virtually no rest, I was then picked up by Area Two detectives and placed in a line-up so rigged that I felt that I was the cargo on an 18 wheeler. (I had no idea how corrupt the Area Two were; they were the infamous headquarters where torture was systematic and its commander Jon Burge was sentenced to five years in prison for perjury, though the men they electro-shocked in the testicles; the men they suffocated with typewriter bags; the men they beat while covering their bodies with phonebooks to conceal or minimize bruising all spent, on average, twenty years in prison for the abuse).

A man saw my photo in the newspaper for the July 3rd murder and told the police that I looked like the guy who killed his friend; the fact that I was six inches shorter, 60-90 pounds lighter and five-to-nine years younger made no difference. I was the only one in the line-up with long braided hair; of no mention of long hair did any witness initially speak. The police were so convincing that I actually began to think that I may have actually killed this guy, but once they said it was a .357 revolver, I knew therein lied my exoneration. I couldn't keep track of all the people I shot, but I could take confidence in my innocence because I never used revolvers.

I guess since the police told Taniacka they'd get me because they wanted me, so now they had me, so there would be no escape.

All of my life I had thought I would dodge jail if I was captured by death. I knew that murder or prison was a rite of passage in the

Chicago streets, but I felt if I sought my murder diligently enough it would negate my imprisonment: God was I wrong. I never asked myself "what have I gotten myself into?", but this seemed surreal. I never even thought that while being shot at, but this was because I was from an area that fed off of one another like vultures and the rotting corpses of the slain soldier who was picked apart by the vultures. Oddly, as we fed off of each other by "eating" each other's future with bullets, the system salivates banging its hands on the table with its gavel screaming, "MORE MEAT" like an intellectual zombie prior to devouring us in the form of a prison cell.

This caused me to be more hurt than angry; I was ascribed the culpability for someone else's murder, and who can accept that without the psychological torture to come with it? This pain was eating at me like a great white shark bite that eviscerates an injured seal that's trapped in its razor sharp teeth. Even prior to this current dilemma, I was fueled by anger and pain, but now I had no way to channel it in the direction of others, so I began to internalize it more than it ever should be. Though I spent about three months in the Audy Home, it was like a blur. The days were monotonous; I'd wake up and spend an hour reading the Bible I had taken from the hospital that mom had brought on one of her visits; I'd exercise for an hour; I'd stretch for an hour and wash up only to repeat the cycle for the 18 hours I was awake throughout the day. On two nights a week, we were allowed to go into the TV room with a supervisor, but I rarely opted to go because I knew that my 17th birthday was going to send me to the adult jail, so I chose to stay in the room and brood and ponder and prepare for what I thought the adult jail would be: violent and depraved.

I was trying to stay mentally busy while there to stop from realizing what was being done to me. I had only a vague idea of how much my ancestry was hated, but the animus went much deeper than what even I could fathom. I was essentially being set up for a legal lynching. I was also focusing on trying to change, but it dawned on me that sheer will power wasn't going to cut it; after all, I couldn't stop drinking for more than two days, so I was weak. But while I was still in the Audy Home I was being transported back and forth to a Michael Reese Hospital for check-ups for the wires in my jaw. I met this nurse, C.S. Lewis (it would be years before I discovered this was a pseudonym for famed author, of such important works such as *The Chronicles of Narnia*, *The Screwtape Letters*, and *God in the Dock*, amongst dozens of other writings).

She used to take me from the guards who brought me in shackled from head to toe, and tell them, "Take those off of him; they mess up the reading of the machine." (They didn't). I guess she was saddened by the sight of a skinny little black boy lead around on a leash with as much disdain as any rabies infested pit bull. The faces of all the parents looking as if I were a pedophile on steroids, all while they shielded their kids from me as if I could get to them.

She'd have me in the room and tell me, "Christ loves you no matter what you may have done." That hit me like a ton of bricks, even more than Tanieka's words of "loving me forever", I didn't even bother to try to tell her I was innocent. I felt vulnerable for the first time, but I suppose that once you get down to the crux of my being I was still a kid, minus the bravado, minus the jewelry, minus the guns, wanting to be loved and lashing out with violence in order to attain acceptance, which I deemed a viable substitute.

Can Never Be The Same

Her letters were encouraging and more meaningful than the guys telling me that the "block wasn't the same without me", as if they had no idea that the block was complicit on why I was no longer on it. But though their attempts were appreciated, they meant little.

I kept recalling the hospital trips while I was still in the J.D.C. and how the C/Os would reluctantly comply to her request of removing my cuffs. I did enjoy the mobility in my hands, but the "mobility" in my heart bothered me because of the words she spoke to me. I couldn't fathom a love from someone that I had never met, but she told me Christ did love me. I didn't know this then, but it was my ingrained depravity battling with a spiritual awakening. I didn't want to accept that because I felt only regret for the 16 years I had been on earth.

Tanieka's letters meant more than the guy's letters, but they seemed to only compound an already tortured psyche. I was mad at myself because upon my arrest I had told her to leave me because I had no way of seeing from beneath the blanket of criminal charges.

She said, "I meant it when I said I can't live without you." In hindsight, she was only 14 years old so I didn't want to bind her to me; it wasn't as if I didn't mess up enough people's lives. But she decided to stay and now I had grown accustomed to her affections and didn't want the ties to be severed. I was glad she felt so strongly, but I felt guilt for her being hurt by my situation; this seemed to give credence to the notions my father had of me as being unworthy of being loved. I had grown to believe that he was right and this bothered me even more because if he and I ever agreed on something, this clearly meant my psychopathy was in much need of medication.

During one of my trips to the hospital, "C.S. Lewis" was trying to console me after I told her Taniacka had lost our baby during the first trimester because she was jumped by three girls. I was hurt because she was hurt from the child loss, but I was actually jealous of the fetus. It didn't have to see a world so cruel towards its people, nor did it have to endure the things I had been through. But I was even happier because I didn't have to worry about trying to be a father from prison. I spared the child life long psychological damage. Nor did I have to worry about the cruelty from the world in general. But I never told her (or anyone) that for fear of how it may have sounded. I had long felt that the words of rapper Gangsta Nip saying, *"Been poor all my life...so I reached for the sky. I regret I was born...and I can't wait till I die."* (*Southpark Psycho*: "Actions *Speak Louder Than Words*"). Even though I wasn't guilty of one of the murders; even though I didn't pull the trigger on the other murder, I felt guilt nonetheless for the loss of this child because I wasn't there to protect her. But in all honesty, my birth implicated my guilty feelings.

My mother and Oscar were crucial to my not giving up completely, but the love I felt from them was powerful enough to help me seek God in order to be better for them. I had grown determined to be a better son than I had been up unto that point. My violent predilections were aging my mother each second in what should have taken years. I figured that only God could accomplish this. He had to save me from me because I had long known that I was my own worst enemy, thus the need for my eradication was strictly from a self-preservation stand-point (if that makes sense). If I were gone, my biggest antagonist would be gone; my confusion would no longer be an issue. Plus, I wouldn't be weighed down by the guilt of my unborn child; I felt it was paying for the sins of its father, so I wanted to minimize my sins so that I wouldn't lose anyone else. I wanted to think progressively and most certainly not as the reactionary as I once was.

Although the Chicago streets were comparable to the surface of the sun, I was removed from it only to be placed in a vat of acid in order to putrify my already imperfect flesh by my placement in the adult Cook County Jail. November 13, 1993 was the day the state waited for. My 17th birthday relegated me to adult status; this merely from a judicial standpoint because I had long thought I was an adult. Since I started drinking, selling dope, having sex, and shooting at people, I figured I was grown. But now, the system was telling me that I *will* be punished like one. I had to take my "medicine" like a man. And in so doing, I had forfeited my prom plan and senior year of high school. But as unconcerned I was about graduating, I planned on doing so (if I lived) in order to please mom; it was the least I could do for her. Emil was going to let me drive his '93 Cadillac to prom, but now I was being "chaperoned" by guards with shotguns and mini-assault rifles on my way to the county.

After being transported with hundreds of guys in the process of being housed in misery, the degradation would now begin. Our processing entailed every orifice being searched, plus the C/Os proved their cowardice by their tough talk. I had long found out that the bigger the mouth, odds were, the smaller the heart. I was given a reprieve of sorts because they knew that I was coming from the J.D.C.

One of the guards told me, "Hey kid, whatever you do, don't drop the soap." This was hysterical to his fellow guards; it dawned on me that maybe if they found the potential rape of a 17 year old funny, then maybe they were the depraved ones. I didn't respond, I just gave him a look telling him, "If I could, I would kill you" and he immediately stopped grinning. He said to his fellow guards, "Oh, this a tough one. Let's see how long he lasts." I briefly gave credence to their comments, but I quickly realized that I had nothing to fear because I knew that if it bled I could kill it. I tuned them out; their voice became white noise; sounds on a radio station when the reception is bad...chchchchch.

I made it to the tier at about 10:00 p.m. so everyone was locked up in their cells. There was a large control room where the guard sat; there were eight steel tables with six steel seats; there were six steel benches about ten feet long to watch TV from, and the TV was about four feet in the air from the benches. All one had to do was stand on the first bench and change the channel. I don't know why I wasn't scared, but even had I been this would have caused me to be extra precautious. I couldn't really rest, though I closed my eyes wondering what would tomorrow bring or hoping that God didn't bring it, at least not for me.

The next day, as I sat at the small desk in the cell responding to a letter I received on my last day in the J.D.C. someone threw some water in our cell and I instinctively got up and went out of the cell screaming, "Whoever did it is a b#!<?h-ass nigga." I stood waiting for someone to approach to try to fight, but no one came. A G.D. named "Fuss" came over to me and said, "What you is?" (What gang am I in). After I told him he said, "Lil' folks, that b#!<ch word a get you killed in here." I never considered that because I used that word often towards guys who I was mad at without any consequence.

I never thought about that because I was always under the premise that I could defend myself (or my guns would defend me). Fuss talked to me for awhile giving me jail "do's and don'ts". He told me never accept anything from anybody because they may want to be repaid with a "favor" that I didn't want to give. He also told me that the first sign of disrespect (What counts as disrespect varies on the person) hit the person as hard as you could or with something, or stab him. This was always at the forefront of my mind. I found out it was one of the B.G.s who threw the water on me by mistake because he was aiming for my cellmate. I apologized to him and he said he knew I just came from the J.D.C. so he didn't respond like he normally would.

This was the type of silliness we contended with on the school wing that I was placed on. One second the different gangs were playing cards or dominoes with one another, the next minute they were trying to kill each other. And oddly, they'd revert back to playing with one another again. I was shocked because I held grudges; I was still mad at my dad for not secreting me on a sheet. I guess the immaturity on the school wing was pretty much a microcosm of the immaturity and dangerous aspect of guys from our communities. Though I was the youngest guy on the tier, it was created for 17-21 year olds.

The Lost Boys

I hadn't been on the tier a full three days before I endured my first riot. I don't know the catalyst of it, but it was either someone drunk all of the Kool-aid at lunch (I'm serious); someone owed a debt from gambling, or someone wanted to watch something on the TV that someone else didn't. Suffice it to say, it could have been actually avoided. But here you had a melting pot of guys from different gangs, facing centuries in prison and unable to lash out at the courts and judges who were really "disrespecting" them, so it was internalized and distributed among each other. We had no natural sedatives; we had no natural sexual release; we had nothing natural but violence.

How could we not seek it? I was fortunate to not be a victim of murder because of reasons unknown. During this instance, a Latin King tried to stab me; the simple fact that he was almost "wind- milling" allowed for me to know, from which direction it was going to come, so I shifted to the left and hit him in the jaw. But then Fuss pushed me out of the way and started fighting him; he disarmed the guy and beat him severely, only sustaining a superficial laceration. I promptly went and fought an unarmed opposition until the guards swarmed the tier with tear gas and in full riot gear.

We spent a couple weeks on "lockdown", but when we came off I asked Fuss when were we going to retaliate. He said, "Lil' folks it ain't nothing. It's a part of jail." I couldn't fathom that to not retaliate was like not exhaling carbon dioxide. My entire criminal life was a pretext only for retaliation for any infraction (real or imagined). I felt that their attack was a sign of "disrespect" and I didn't want to accept it. But far be it for me to tell Fuss how to do jail time. Fuss was a 19 year old who had just been released from the juvenile Department of Corrections (prison). He was gone since he was 15 until he was 17 and then locked back up for the murder charge he was fighting (he would be acquitted two years later).

I discovered that there were plenty of opportunities for us to shed each others blood, and they were taken advantage of. The closest I had ever been to death in jail took place a few weeks after the last riot. There were two B.D.s on the tier and we were surrounded by 15-20 oppositions (people under the 5 point star, though G.D.s were often our antagonists as well). B.D. had called one of their guys the dreaded b#$¢h word. I was trying to arrange it so that those two could fight it out; man-to-man combat. And if that was a Hollywood script, they probably would have. But once an individual sees that the numbers are in their favor, all man-to-man combat is relegated to mythical status. I know that once blood is wanted, it had to be spilled, but I was not going to allow for it to be ours (I tried).

Once I noticed that the talk was going nowhere, I promptly hit the closest one to me. His nose started bleeding profusely, and at this time one of them hit me in the head with a "soap sock" (sock filled with bars of soap) and I was slightly dazed. I then grabbed the one bleeding and dragged him from the shower area that we were in, because if I was going to die, I wanted the G.D.s to see it. It was me and one B.D. fighting all of those guys for what seemed like an eternity, but mostly those guys were hitting each other trying to get at us, and I wasn't letting my "prey" go unless they pulled him from "my cold dead hands" like Charleston Heston claimed. When you are forced to fight for your physical life, the physical strength one could muster is amazing. The G.D.s came to help reluctantly after Fuss told them," I ain't gonna let lil' folks get killed."

The G.D.s and B.p.s had long had an ambivalent relationship. The catalyst was over 30 years old because once the King of the Black Gangster Disciple Nation died it went to crap. Larry Hoover wanted to be the king; Booney Black wanted to be the king; Jerome "Shorty" Freeman wanted to be the King. And since there would be no sharing of power, they split into 3 "factions" if you will. Larry branched off to rule the G.D. s, Booney to rule the B.G.s, and "Shorty" branched off to rule the B.D.s. So though we spawn from the same tree, there is a great deal of dysfunction in it. What family isn't dysfunctional?

The fact that at 150 pounds and 17 years old, I fought off an entire mob with such ferocity that even the G.D.s that I knew hated me were receptive of me (not that I wanted it). I simply was fighting for my life, but I didn't know that at the time that "if God be for me, who then can be against me?" (Romans 8:28). They told me the simple fact that I wasn't scared to enter the shower area swayed them (briefly) over to being of any assistance. But just like family, they too had short memories. Fortunately, I was leery of their flattering comments of, "Man, lil' folks, you a real nigga." I knew that they were as trustworthy as a rabies-infested pit bull; their love and hatred of me swung like a metronome.

It seemed that my quest for God went no further than reading the Bible and going to church. The problem with my church attendance was that it was more focused on handling gang affairs than it was to find God. The heads of the gang required us to supply them with the number of B.D.s on the tier, the number of every opposition on the tier and other inconsequential information. I had missed the solitude of the J.D.C. I was too interested in shooting craps and drinking "hooch" (jail made liquor) than I was concerned with God. This concoction of oranges, bread, sugar and about a week fermenting was indulged in to try to negate the horrible state of my jail life; I found it odd because this was precisely what I had been contending with prior to incarceration. I kept trying to drink away my problems regardless of the fact that it doesn't work.

This caused me a great deal of frustration over my lack of zeal for the "things of God" as I understood it. I kept Wondering if the Bible was for me at all. I had no idea that I was in the process of being "broken" by God, which I found ironic because I had always felt that I was broken, but this had to happen in order for me to be made "whole" and hopefully in this process I wouldn't be shattered. The ten months I spent in division ten on its school wing was alright I suppose, for jail, but since I had never spent more than a night in custody I didn't have much to compare it to. We were able to watch movies at school and listen to rap music, so it was more tolerable than the other tiers in the jail. No one could have foreseen our relocation.

It was about 7:00 a.m. this August morning and the guards told about 22 of us on the school wing to pack up our belongings because we were going to be moved to another division. It was because a riot transpired on another school wing and it proved fatal so in the powers that were, they decided to swap dozens of guys from the 3 double max security school wings; it was essentially like a game of "duck, duck, goose" where you really didn't know where you were going to end up.

This taught me that to be "comfortable" while incarcerated is an oxymoron.

I believe the Superintendent's logic was flawed because it didn't matter where he put us because as long as he received individuals in our age range and with similar cases another fatal riot was always on the verge of happening. We waited in a holding area ("bullpen") for several hours before we made it to our respective tier. My first reaction to the tier was that it looked like a scene from *American Me*. The place was huge in comparison to the division we left; division 9 tiers each had a top and bottom gallery with 29 cells each capable of holding two people per cell. And as daunting as the place seemed, it was the huge puddle of dried blood from where one of the two fatalities occurred that made me really ponder the seriousness of incarceration; as if my fighting my way out of a similar fate not long before the move didn't. I was housed with a guy named Joe. He was 22 years old, technically too old to be on the school wing, but a bed in jail was a bed to the administration.

After they finally let us out, I saw one of the B.G.s from 103rd and Wentworth. "Meathead" (So called because of the extra layers of skin on his neck) was a welcomed sight. It wasn't that he and I were so close, but that he was from the land, so I gravitated towards him. Plus, Terrance had introduced us once when I spent an excessive amount of time over there. Though our gang ties were close, this wasn't going to stop me from helping one of the B.D.s murder him for his involvement in the death of his friend. The fact that he was locked up so quickly after the murder (about two days before me) was the reason he survived.

I was glad we didn't get a chance to kill him because I found out he had nothing to do with the murder, he too was simply a victim of the "Accountability Theory" which punished mostly people from my demographic (see 720 Illinois Compiled Statute 5-8-1 (a) (c) (ii)), we clearly had more loyalty to one another than to the other folks.

The dynamics of this school wing were better than division ten's; we actually were studying for our G.E.D. I suppose the teachers in division nine thought that since we were facing centuries in prison, why should they bother trying to educate us. We weren't on this school wing long before the oddest of situations transpired. I was playing cards with Meathead when about 60 or so S.O.R.T (Special Operations Response Team) bumrushed the tier in full riot gear forcing guys into their cells with their dogs which had been trained to dislike people who looked like me. I could understand the need for billy clubs, helmets, tear gas and shields had a riot taken place, but this (then) seemed unnecessary. I would find out the reason: the jail had grown over crowded so they tried to implement a third man to a cell policy, but this didn't go over well to the guys on the tier they tested it on. They decided to use force to put us in our cells, and then bring the third person into the cell.

I hated that often times the guys forced to be placed in the cell was often times beat up or raped by their cellmates as if tearing him down was getting back at the administration who had placed him there. Though the courts would eventually deem this an 8th Amendment violation (cruel and unusual punishment), they were allowed to get away with it for years before someone litigated it in the federal court. I found it embarrassing to have a grown man sleeping on the floor; it couldn't do anything but remind me of the slave ships during the Trans Atlantic slave trade. Ironically, the same heritage that fueled that slavery was now fueling the present 21st century slavery. I guess it's easy since my demographic (heritage) had a tendency to be lost. In our "lost" state, we sought to find ourselves through genocidal acts adding a faux credence to our needing to be incarcerated as we were.

Dungeons... and Dragons

One day Joe and I were in the cell talking, and he decided I was trustworthy enough to show his "shank" (makeshift knife made from whatever was available). His particular shank had a good six inch blade, so properly used it could prove fatal. I asked him, "Why you try'na catch a murder, you got three years." He had recently pled guilty to a drug charge. He was quiet for a minute, but then said, "Man, I ain't try'na catch a murder, but if I gotta stab somebody I'm gone do it." It dawned on me that we placed ourselves in situations that we "had" to jeopardize our futures. I learned this the hard way. I guess when someone offers us daylight we have a tendency to want to stay in the dark. As violently predisposed I was prior to jail, I made a conscious choice to never carry a knife. I was tired of the bloodshed, but I can't say was it because of what it brought me, or was God really doing something internally. I actually discovered that violence wasn't accomplishing as much as I thought it was.

I knew that the tapestry between violence was indifference; I thought it was right because my conscience was emaciated by my own hatred for life. I was taught to show my anger through violence and the angrier I was, the more violent I should behave. This is a lie from the pits of hell. Joe would be shipped out to prison not long after that, but unbeknownst to me his shank would still be there. I had just returned from the commissary, and after winning some "money" from shooting dice (granted money can be anything from cookies, cakes, and cigarettes) I had been informed that my cell had been searched and this shank was found. On November 7, 1994 I would be placed in seg for his knife. As punitive as they may have intended it to be, I found solitude, so I sought God. It seemed that since I went to the adult jail, I really didn't have a chance to "stray" from the folks.

I was caught up in the fray of gang life.

During this time, I noticed that good things (though they didn't feel good) but God was piercing my soul. I had to choose would I lose myself to God or would I lose myself to the gang. The choice wasn't as hard as I thought. I did find difficulties seeing how (why) God would love me when even my dad didn't, but this was always the case.

Chapter 4: The Departed

I decided to leave the gang by taking myself off count (non active) in the gang life. I didn't find those 15 days in seg, nor the fact that I'd spend my 18th birthday in seg, too much of a big deal. I was expecting to be moved to the school wing, but I wasn't. I had been moved to 2-E with my guy Terrance from 103rd. He had been locked back up for an armed robbery. We maneuvered it so that we could be cellmates because the officer who worked the tier smoked and I had an abundance of cigarettes from gambling (I wasn't perfect). Though he didn't try to sabotage my efforts at Christianity, he did tell me that he saw me as I once was. I told him it was my duty to alter that. My visits had still been consistent, so jail wasn't as horrific as it could have been, but I guess on some levels I was still everybody's "baby brother".

I received letters from everybody I didn't see; T.R. was sending me some of the money I had left with him from my "get a car fund" since I'd spend it up had I kept it. This December 22, 1994 date will too forever go down in my "history book" of tragedies. It was a Thursday and T.R. and Roy had come up to visit me and he told me that he had gotten into an altercation with Bobby and the G.D.s over the "Deen".

He said he pulled his Mac 10 and they promptly dispersed. He told me he hadn't come to see me in awhile because no criminal wants to go to his potential destination; it was a jinx. I definitely understood that logic. I told him that Bobby was a "snake" and that he should have given me the green light for his murder before my incarceration. He agreed, but I also told him to be careful because when someone pulls a gun on you and don't use it, it's a street code to pull yours on them and to make sure you use it.

We chilled for an hour, and he told me, "See you next week." But he wouldn't. He wouldn't see anyone else again... except for his killer.

I called home at about 8:00 p.m. and told my sister Sylvia I had just seen T.R. and I noticed she was quiet. These non-familial visits always gave me happiness family visits didn't; it was because family was bound by blood to see you, but not friends. Or so I thought then. She somberly said, "Marcos, Jamie got killed tonight." I convinced her this was impossible because I just saw him. She told me that after Roy dropped him off in front of his house, Bobby had some kid waiting for him in the driveway. He was shot dead like a dog in the street and I felt it was my fault because had he not came to visit me he would've been able to stay guarded.

On many levels I had thought he was invincible because he had been shot four times in 1992, leaving his left arm permanently crippled.

In his underestimation of Bobby, he lost his life. And instead of contemplating the birth of Christ, I was contemplating the murder of Bobby.

I found nothing ironic about plotting his murder while fighting two charges already. I kept telling myself and Terrance that I should've killed Bobby, knowing T.R. wanted him spared. Those feelings were compounded with each look at the obituary after I got it. The story got even sadder because I found out some 15 year old would get arrested and ultimately receive 35 years for the murder. Bobby would flee town after a couple of attempts were made on his life by T.R.'s Vice Lord brothers.

While my dejection over T.R.'s murder lingered, I was called to go back to the school wing. I was ambivalent because I didn't want to leave my guy Terrance. He would plea out to five years plus three for his crime. He told me before I left the tier, "Family, if you gone do the Christian thing, don't fake it. I hate guys when they fake it." I told him I had no intention of faking it. I hugged my brother and left for the school wing and all of the adolescent ways I wanted to get back to. In my defense, I had no idea that I would find myself ritually involved with the folks. I knew deep in my heart that it would cost me, but I didn't know what I would be forced to pay. Or could I afford it? It happened so subtlety; one moment I was simply praying with them over their food, the next, I was involving my input in gang business I had thought I didn't care about. It tormented me because I thought myself severing the ties, but some way they were "stitched" together again.

The Price Is Life

On April 24, 1995, I went to my first murder trial. As the Public Defender and Prosecutor waded through about forty prospective jurors, I felt the judgmental glares from them long before any evidence was put forth about the case. Four people testified that they saw me kill this man, but three of them didn't have any description of the killer on the night in question. The only witness standing one foot away told the police he was at least 6' 1" tall;180-220 pounds and 20-25 years old. I, at the time of trial was merely 5'9 and that came since my incarceration. I was 5'6, 130 pounds and 16 when I supposedly committed this murder. It got better, there were two witnesses who said the killer touched the driver's side door handle; the prints would prove not to be mine, but the witnesses perjured themselves by saying they never told the police that. But that wasn't the only perjury they'd, commit. They also told the jury they didn't say the killer was "that big."

I suppose that to the jury (of none of my peers), my long hair was nothing but the epitomization of a "thug" so could I have really expected any other verdict? There were several other questionable components, such as the witnesses testifying that they were passing around the photo of me with a newspaper before the lineup. I may have been too confident but this was because of the illusory notion of "innocent until proven guilty", but it's actually the other way around. I did enjoy seeing mom and Taniacka at trial supporting me, and whatever sibling chose to "bless" me with their presence. Taniacka was pregnant, but far be it from me to care about who she was opening her legs to; she was only 16 or 17 years old. In my foolishness, I really expected an acquittal, but I discovered that "justice" wasn't only blind, but the broad was a racist deaf old lady.

The guilty verdict took over eight hours and a note from the jury said, "They couldn't agree." The judge told them that if they didn't agree, they'd be sequestered to a hotel until they did. It was like they didn't even finish reading the note before they came back with a guilty verdict. I felt this "blackmail" of the jury detracted from any chance of "justice". Clearly, the court wanted its "pound of flesh"; or in my case, its 190 pounds of flesh.

I tried to tell myself that I couldn't allow the jury's empty words (false verdict), nor my own empty feelings fill me with despair. But sadly, it seemed as if this was the only thing I had to "eat".

This conviction instantly relegated me to non-existent because I knew this conviction was merely a precursor to a life sentence that loomed over head because of the multiple murder statute in Illinois (730 111.Comp.Stat.5/5-8 1(a) (c) (i).) I was trying to tell myself to hold on but I felt with this verdict that God had let me go so I had nothing to clutch on to as I fell further into the abyss of incarceration.

I turned to see how this would cause my family to react, but mostly my mom's reaction. I had felt even more guilt over the fact that I seemed to only cause her heartbreak after heartbreak; she had dropped her head and hugged Taniacka while my siblings shook their heads in disgust or disbelief (probably both). The tears on my mom's face broke me more than the verdict, but I was stoic in appearance, as I had taught myself to be. I was a soldier (so I told myself), and I must never let my enemy see me distraught; internally was another matter. I felt like a runaway train on the inside of a crashing 747 diving into the - Pacific Ocean never to be seen again. Essentially, I felt that my conviction was the equivalent to the carnage it caused, but with no opportunity to be salvaged.

I had long known that being a representative of a socio-economically depressed demographic wouldn't benefit me in the long run, but for some strange reason I acted as if I was oblivious to this fact. The foolishness of believing that my innocence would matter to a jury (of mostly Caucasians) who had never been forced to deal with life and death situations while as a teenager (if at all) was somehow lost on me. I found my proceedings had separated (segregated) me from the prospect of justice because of my "blackness". I found it ironic, while I looked at the American flag behind the judges huge bench; if memory served me correctly it was supposed to safeguard the "constitutional rights" of its citizens, I foolishly believed that my birth in America meant me. It was even more odd looking at the Illinois State flag, with the Eagle holding a shield in its talons, yet beneath the shield was an olive branch. This implied peaceful intentions, yet it seemed always ready for war. I was somewhat dazed by the verdict, and now presumably the "stars and stripes" were being transformed into bars and pipes to beat me into correct behavior.

The guilty verdict seems to have echoed long after she spoke it, and it seemed as if the olive branch was removed from the Eagle's mouth, but my squirming body was in its place while the shield in its talons impaled me while screaming GUILTY all the while. I had no way to combat the villainy that I had been subjected to due to geographical and ancestral designations. As honest as I was becoming to myself regarding the need for my imprisonment since I wasn't able to find death, I couldn't fathom the incarceration as having to come behind an injustice propagated as fact simply to solve a murder case. It seemed so permanent, but I would find out that injustice wasn't as uncommon as I thought; I wasn't an anomaly. I felt as if the "scales of justice" were weighing me and I was found wanting (lacking) of a soul worth saving, or a life worth living. I was found wanting of innocence that I shouldn't have lost (or maybe I forfeited it). I was essentially found to be lacking the requirements of being human. I was like an infected animal deserving the quarantine called prison to preserve the whole of society from being infected because of my presence.

All of my life I had been forced to hear about a place that I thought I would never see: prison. I strongly felt that I was the perfect contestant for a game of death, so I wouldn't see it. I strongly felt that I was a prime candidate to be elected as a murder victim; so I wouldn't see it. Sadly, as with most of my beliefs, or decisions, I made the tactical error by concluding that I would escape prison via death. Though my peers viewed prison with pride, I didn't share that sentiment because I didn't like existing before incarceration, but at least in the streets there were amenities to distract one from how miserable life was, considering I felt I had no intrinsic value. I was now lost to a "kidnapping" under the threat of never being freed.

I was sentenced on June 15, 1995, but prior to sentencing they have a pre-sentencing procedure to theoretically assess what sentence should be given. They twisted every word I said and made it seem as if I were incorrigible. Like when I stated I "had a disdain for life", they reported "I had a disregard for human life" or when I stated "I hated my dad", they stated "I hated authority figures." I did hate that my mother and sister, Toya, attempted to sway the judge by the fact that I was maltreated by my father and the fact that my alcoholism made matters worse; it didn't matter because the judge gave me 55 years and 30 years (only five years less than the maximum), so I may as well have told the court, "F#*fc you" and I couldn't have gotten anything but five more years. But in my mind, this bogus murder could have yielded 20 years as a sentence (the minimum) but it didn't offset the error of it.

This conviction was literally the worst thing to have happened to me, minus being born, but I felt I still didn't deserve that.

Here I sat, 18 years old with half a century as a prison sentence still facing a few more centuries because of another trial that would shortly be underway. I knew that the Bridgeview Courthouse was salivating over their turn to impart to me the disdain of an entire nation, but I had no reinforcements to help me fight off a system that had been abusing its powers since its inception. And my belief that God was my aid didn't help at all.

For anyone who has ever been convicted for murder, especially the innocent, it's like someone took a shovel and began digging your insides out all the way from the heart to the intestines. The anguish is indescribable, leaving you physically and mentally weak.

I can say that all of my desires to die pre-incarceration were compounded by that verdict; but no one would know. I was further tortured because once I was able to see my mom, she said the victim's dad didn't even believe that I killed his son. I found it uncanny that the victim's dad could see this, but the jury couldn't; they just didn't want to.

A couple of the guys on the tier with me asked did I "blame God" for my conviction, because despite my obvious flaws, I was sincere with Him. I told them "no", but secretly I did blame Him. I tried not to let that verdict dictate my thoughts, so I studied for my G.E.D. in hopes of being distracted—it didn't work. I felt that progression was pointless and that my life was only crap now finally being flushed down a toilet called prison (since I knew this would be my destination).Once I was forced to face my own culpability, it wasn't as excruciating, but the injustice still lingered in my psyche. I didn't know this then, but God's blessings come in His time and in His ways, so amid the obstacles I was going through, I would have to persevere.

It was extremely hard for me to write Tanieka telling her that I would ALWAYS love her, but that she must go. I then took her letters and photos and promptly set them ablaze in the cell's sink. I didn't do it out of malice, but I had to focus on the next phase of my existence, and she didn't need to be in it.

I hadn't fully digested the last conviction before being placed back in the gauntlet for another jury trial. On December 4, 1995 I chose my jury, which was a task in and of itself considering this victim was a Caucasian woman. I can only imagine that, based upon the numerous negative media reports, they would've opted to grab a noose, an old sturdy oak tree and handed down "justice" in a Jim Crow era type of penalty: lynching. I supposed that they would have to deal with a "legal lynching" instead, where the black robe of the judge would take the place of the KKK's white one, and the gavel would operate as the noose. The trial was short and simple: my prints matched those found on the victim's car and an incriminating statement was given after five hours of police interrogation without my pain medication from the broken jaw suffered a couple days prior (the Appellate Court would reverse conviction because the police denied my mom access to me, though she was present).

I was not expecting to be spirited from the jail's holding area by a "special escort" of two tactical team members. I was literally placed on a maintenance vehicle that they drive to get around the jail and rushed to segregation. I asked the officer why was this happening and he said, "You guys who get sentences like that are automatically on suicide watch." I always wondered how my buddies on the school wing were doing, because far as I saw it, they were the best group of guys to be around during this trying moment. About an hour after I was in segregation, a psychiatrist, Dr. Stein, came and spoke with me. She asked me, "How do you feel?" I wanted to ask her how would she feel if someone took her from a pit of lava (the streets) and then dropped her in a vat of acid, while injecting her with adrenaline to keep her alive so that she could keep enduring the pain, but I didn't. I told her that I would be back on appeal so it didn't matter.

She arched her eyebrow, but after a few more moments of being as composed as I possibly could, she gave me a clean bill of health (I know right?) Though she told me my faith in God was commendable, she also told me it was probably a waste of energy. I wondered how ill conceived her plan was to tell a 19 year old that had been given life in prison that his faith in God was a waste. I posited that she was an idiot. I kept thinking about the irony in my mother trying to get me to see a "shrink" prior to my incarceration, but if this woman was any indication on the adeptness of someone helping me with obvious mental issues, I was glad that I didn't go and see one. Before she left though, she said, "You're an interesting young man Mr. Gray. I hope you'll be alright." I thanked her, but didn't know could I believe her. I guess she was just expecting to see me ranting and raving, or at the least crying. I would not give her the pleasure.

As I laid in "seg" thinking about the day's events, it dawned on me that I was tired. I wasn't just tired of being awoke, but tired of being alive. Granted, this feeling had been a part of my psyche for so long that I simply had grown used to it, but I really pondered putting the shoelaces to work that the idiots had left me with. But the thought would be that "they" won; "they" defeated me by causing me to defeat me. Even in my self inflicted death, I couldn't live with that.

I continued to wrestle with that thought all night, but I was convinced that since God had made me a "new creation" I couldn't just cop out to suicide because of the pain I was in. At least, on some levels I was able to prepare for the pain. But that was strictly from a theoretical standpoint because practically I couldn't take it.

I thought of Nelson Mandela, who had spent 27 years imprisoned and that was from strictly political issues, but on some levels I did deserve incarceration, but for the rest of my life? I was trying to recall any Bible verse to help me then. I remembered, "All things work together for the good of those who loved God and was called according to His purpose." (Romans 8:28); I recalled, "No weapon formed against me shall prosper, and every false tongue spoken against me shall be condemned." (Isiaih 54:17).

Despite my imperfections, I wanted to be of some use to God because I wasn't totally oblivious to the blessings He had given me prior to and during incarceration. I felt compelled to pray more sincerely than even when I was going to trial. I discovered that it was one thing to request from God a blessing of freedom, but it was totally different to ask Him to strengthen you as you lay in a viper's nest sent there by your own foolishness and a systems corruption. I asked for God to show me the "purpose" of my circumstance because I knew that it wasn't just to cause me to have to fight even more vigorously against suicide.

God told me that despite my horrid past and my abysmal present, that I had a better future waiting for me if I trusted Him. And true to Marcos, I argued with Him telling Him that I wanted it "NOW" and not after I die and go to heaven. It was like I trusted God in increments; half of the day He had it, the other portion I tried to figure out what would happen. As I wrestled with this throughout the night, I noticed that it was about 7:00 a.m. and I was told that I would be moved out of seg and on to 1-E. I almost felt that I would miss seg because it was there where I am always sparked to think more in depth regarding my relationship with God.

I expected that my decision to sever my gang ties was not going to be well received . I knew that being in their clutches and then trying to leave could have yielded violent consequences; because the gangs actually survived because of its members. This is especially true from an incarceration standpoint; the individual numbers offered presumed protection for the collective membership. They were more than willing at times, to inflict violence upon others, for deciding to leave; I personally had been used as an instrument to exact this penalty on members for perceived infractions, I wondered would I be violated for my decision to leave them; I also wondered would I fight back when the time came (as instinct dictates). The odd thought came making me wonder would I die by the hands of the gang that I swore to die for at 14 years old. I really figured that the things (or persons) that we love the most could hurt us the deepest.

As all of those thoughts came to mind, I was instructed to leave the tiny 9x6 cell so that they could consider my request (which felt like my jury was deliberating).

I knew that they were also considering whether or not I would receive the violation as a "going away" present. I felt that if I had to shed blood in order to gain freedom from the bondage of gang membership, then so be it. My Savior (Christ) shed His life's blood for me, so I had to be willing to return the favor.

As I sat waiting for the gang hierarchy's decision, I wondered would I be acquitted of betraying the gang or would they convict me of the perceived disloyalty that would have yielded a violation as a sentence. I know that some wanted this because of my decision, but the thing that compelled me the most was the feeling that I was a hypocrite by claiming Christian, disobeying God while affiliated with a street gang.

Though the system and the prison administration would forever relegate me to a gang banger, I was trying to figure out how I was going to identify myself without the stigma of being a gang banger. I was blessed by God to have not having to deal with any physical ramifications for leaving the gang; I had drawn my line in the sand and after having stepped on to the other side, I was now going to try to disregard the erroneous ideals I held prior to incarceration. The gang culture desensitized me to what was right or wrong.

It was cool on 1-E. The guards would open the door to our cell because of the favor my cellmate had with him. It would be after the 11:00 p.m. count, when everyone was supposed to be in their cells.

He'd tell us to maneuver the couches so that we couldn't be seen as we watched TV from the guard post. Granted, we'd have to feed 58 guys their breakfast the next morning, but it was a small price to pay for a little extra "freedom" from the cell. Also one of the B.G.'s leaders was over there with us. This brought perks I couldn't have imagined (or needed) as well. He'd send us all money, but there wasn't ever too many so it didn't matter, but he also would get weed and alcohol in for us.

I admit that I indulged in the grain alcohol he got in specifically for me, but instead of my usual violent rampages after drinking, I simply sat in the cell wallowing in depression. It dawned on me that I was depressed enough without the alcohol, so I wouldn't drink again. My cellmate, Eddie, was a B.D. that I knew from the school wing who had went to seg for a knife. He swore by the B.G. "chief" Sonny. I noticed that he tried to buy loyalty, but I, as broke as I was, knew that loyalty couldn't be bought because the moment you stop paying all that you've done would be quickly forgotten.

I would eventually move out of the cell with Eddie 'because he was drawing closer to the gang while I was trying to sever all ties.

Moving On Up

After a few months on 1-E, I was able to move back upstairs to the school wing. The tier had a lot of new faces, but there were some old ones as well. I noticed that the tension was thick immediately between the opposite gangs and I found my way right in the middle of it. One day after we came from school for lunch at 11:00 a.m. the brothers launched a sneak attack against the folks. I was in the shower washing out my shirt because I spilled juice on it and a VL came in there swinging wildly. He caught me, ever so slightly, on the jaw, and I immediately went into feral mode; I hit him in the face with the wet shirt and then hit him in the nose and after that, he was done. He keeled over and I began to beat him like he gave me the life sentence until God tapped me on the shoulder asking me, "Do you want to kill him?"

I stopped and left the shower before any of the guards bumrushed the tier.

My cellmates DeSean and Eddie G. (G.D.'s from the area) were pissed. They plotted revenge before the wounds were even healed. I was still thinking about how close I was to killing a guy for no reason; granted it was self-defense initially, but it grew into revenge. I heard that Sonny was acquitted and murdered promptly after release. The streets are cruel like that at times. All the while, I'm listening to DeSean plot the murder of one of the VL's he didn't like. I was trying to talk him down, but can you tell a pit bull not to bite after it's been ordered to? I stopped trying.

I was allowed to move to the school wing because I was 19, but this Sgt. investigated why I wasn't there in the first place and after discovering my sentence of 999 years (it actually said that), she moved me from the school wing as if I were the reason it had recently rioted. She said, "You're too dangerous to be on the school wing" as if the school wing was inhabited by baby unicorns and pink pandas. I told Eddie G. and DeSean to be cool, all the while knowing they would not, because once you seek revenge, it's the only thing to calm you.

Not long after that talk, I approached the B.D.'s chief and explained to him my intentions. I said, "I need to drop my flags because I can't keep claiming I'ma Christian still gangbanging." I noticed he had an inquisitive look, but he said, "Folks, you know I can have you violated. But I be seeing you in the Bible all day, I know you ain't playing. You got our blessing. A verse came to mind, "when the ways of a man are pleasing to God, He makes even His enemies be at peace with him." (Proverbs 16:7). I was waiting only for that to translate into my court proceedings. I had grown tired of the vengeful thoughts; I had grown tired of the retaliation against my life in the form of death, which is what gang activity was.

I continued to listen to the "old timers" school me on the ways prison worked. However, a lot of times I noticed that they were only men chronologically because they too had foolish tendencies. I was glad for my soul's shift deeper towards God, which allowed for my gang membership to be as dead as the people I was accused of killing or helping to kill. I was able to "see" my future in the faces of these old men and it scared me, but it was lessened when I viewed it through the eyes of God. I also was enjoying my time with a C/O that I met, who had the capacity to make that hell seem heavenly; but not at first.

Since I was so impressionable, I guess we may never know how this impacted my mental development. The violence that I LOVED hearing in rap songs would eventually surface. I often envisioned doing the same things they spoke about; it's so enmeshed in my psyche that over 20 years later I recall all of the violent lyrics. A small sample of the depravity that I subjected myself to: *"...you think this is harsh, this ain't as harsh as it gets... there's no telling what's being thought of in the mind of a lunatic; my girls getting skinny, she's strung out on dope...so I went to her mother's house and cut out her throat; her grandma was standing there, she was screaming out Brad...she reached for the telephone so I put the blade on granny's ass...went to the back to grab a shovel; now granny's on her way to meet the devil."* (Geto Boys-*Mind Of A Lunatic*).These type of lyrics pervaded (or perverted) my adolescent mind, but essentially these were my choices to make.

I'm sure that everyone incarcerated ponders just how (and why) did their life turn out the way it did. I seemed to have forsaken my family prior to incarceration for a group of people who would eventually show me what I meant to them: nothing. I willingly departed my mother's warming emotional braces only to grab the streets by the hands to find myself clutched by a prison cell. So to whom belongs the blame?

Even while feeling this way, I still sought to get back to the school wing, but I had being growing close to a C/O Mrs. Parker. She was a 35 year old who had worked the tier five days a week. I wasn't physically attracted to her initially; she was about 5'0 tall, somewhat overweight, but she was cute in a sense. We initially had only cordial talks, but she would always commend me for being studious in regards to my case. This opened the door to discuss current events; this opened the door for personal lives, which clearly affections would find their way in. It had soon gotten to a point that I would no longer be able to resist her inner beauty and its strength. I found this a welcomed pleasantry, whereas I was surrounded by bitterness all day.

Though I was placed on a school wing, it wasn't three-A as I wanted it to be. And for some odd reason the guys on this school wing viewed me as if I were the main character in a play. I knew that some of those guys up there knew about my prison sentence, so I was the "car crash" that they couldn't look away from. I guess they saw me as a living (I use that term loosely) crash and they expected me to "blow up" at any moment. I was the Greek tragedy they'd heard about in school taken directly from Homer's Iliad "...*sing of wrath... the destructive wrath...that brought countless sorrows... and sent many valiant souls of Heroes to Hades*..." This seemed to be how I was viewed; this seemed to be how I felt.

This feeling was odd because I had lived how I lived prior to my incarceration, as did most of the inhabitants of my environment lived: carpe diem. We tried to seize the day because we knew that death was around the corner of every block on every street every second of every day. He was always capable of snatching me up, but for some reason he didn't. Statistically speaking, I only had death or jail waiting for me. I shouldn't be surprised by what I was going through. And with all of my efforts to go to the school wing forgotten about, they then decided to move me over there.

I had grown cool with them by showing them that I was merely another guy from the hood, seeking only to understand God while I fought a system hell-bent on trying to destroy me via prison. The guys I had grown cool with were livid once they found out that a teacher on our school wing had been a member of my retrial jury and that he allowed me to be convicted. Whatever sway he once had with them was destroyed by their knowledge of this fact. Some of the folks had actually wanted to stab him up for, in their words, being "a lying bi*!h who always talked that black power s!#*t". The situation was not made any better by my placement in his class.

I saw that he was spooked when I first walked into his class. He was so leery that it made me feel awkward. On about the third day of this, I asked him if I could speak with him in the hallway. He reluctantly complied; I suppose he figured if it was to happen it would. I didn't think about beating him up for too long before I returned to my senses. I told him that I didn't hold any grudges for his role in my conviction and that I knew he simply succumbed to the pressure. He stood silent for a moment before he began to tear up; I felt more awkward at this point. I preferred that more than him flinching every time I was within two feet of him as he used to do. He wasn't all bad; he'd bring new movies, new rap cassettes and sometimes food for me; though this probably was a way for him to soothe his conscience.

He'd get really emotional when explaining his experiences in Vietnam. He'd often tell us that the Caucasian soldiers treated the African American soldiers worse than the Vietnamese. He said they would sometimes catch the Blacks, but let them go, saying, "This no black man's war." I don't mean to digress, but I couldn't have agreed more. The guys on this school wing didn't gang bang as much as they did on three-A. We'd bring his radio back to the tier on Friday so we could listen to it over the weekend. I know that listening to 2Pac may not have been the wisest of choices I made, but they were the choices I made. I felt I needed a "break" from the G.E.D. studies I was involved in. Taniacka had basically left, but I didn't care because Mrs. Parker was now working over there daily.

I couldn't see how much of a distraction she was, but I couldn't care because on some levels I needed a distraction. I figured that God was displeased with me, but I hoped that he saw I had no choice because how could my 19 year old self be blamed for the imminent weakness? I posited that the unnatural separation of man from woman was a punishment far colder than the climate of Siberia. Thus my inherent loneliness, compounded with the deprivation was far more cruel than any tactic employed by the perpetrators during the Spanish Inquisition, in which no punishment was too brutal: being boiled alive, being tarred and feathered, or being stretched out over the rack until you died in agony. I felt the separation I endured did all of this and more.

My days would eventually be spent with her, and this did not bode well with some of the guys on the tier. They'd ask me, "Why she let you stay from school?" I'd simply reply, something to the effect that I had to clean the tier up because it was dirty, or I was sick. But I promptly sought to distance myself from the conversation. People may not realize that sexual relationships with guards isn't as infrequent as they imagine; it's just easier to disregard their existence. I can't lie, our first encounter had all of my adolescent timidity return because my fear rushed in like a tidal wave. But, she being the mature one, guided the terms of the relationship. I was almost oblivious of the fact that I was a convicted murderer facing a slow moving death penalty: natural life.

The hardest thing for me to do was keep my feelings towards her a secret. Even in my prayers to God, she found her ever present memory with me; it stuck with me like a leech, but I dared not pull it away. I was conscious of the fact that this relationship wasn't pleasing to God, plus it seemed to be a catalyst for other questionable activities. I never needed anything, because between my family and Ms. Parker bringing me things from the "free world" (only food, cosmetics, and candy; I'd never ask for drugs or alcohol) I was well taken care of. This, however, did not stop me from gambling almost every day. I posit it was simply greed making me feel that since I had something everybody in my position would want, then I begin to want what they had. I guess I should have been grateful for the guilt I had, but since I felt my entire life was an exercise in guilt, clearly I didn't mind it. I suppose had I stopped feeling it is when I would really be in a dangerous spiritual condition. There I was calling myself a Christian; to show my age group how God works and there I languished in sin, but I felt that since I loved her I was right.

Our time had been somewhat sacrificed because the teacher was beginning to question why was I missing so many days of school; I could not have expected for them to continually believe that I was "sick" as often as she told them. And to my surprise, even after missing so much school, I was able to pass my G.E.D. test. I was glad to have something tangible from my incarceration, since God's working in my life seemed absent.

I wouldn't have too much time to celebrate this achievement because a couple of weeks later I would be moved to one-E again because of my prison sentence (again). I found it disheartening that not only did this conviction take my life, but it continued to impede my progress.

My progress with Ms. Parker being the main thing I hated, but the alienation I kept dealing with consistently showed me that my individuality was lost; my humanity was lost; I was no longer human, but a cog in the machinations of society on an "island of misfit toys" constructed for people from my demographic. I was supposedly locked away for society's safety, but even locked up alienated from the rest of the occupants of the jail. I felt this justified that the entire ambiance of my life was one of darkness, but yet, a glimmering spark of light constantly tried to force its way through; it came in the form of God's Word: The Holy Bible.

Ms. Parker had opened the cell door (electronically) and told me to come to the interlock (glassed area where C/Os view the tier from, as I was buzzed in, she said, "I'm sorry Marcos, they moving you today." I processed this with the same shock as I did my verdicts, but remained stoic. She had the saddest look in her eyes, and I felt as if spikes were embedded in my ankles dragging me through the same shards of glass I felt I'd been chewing all of my life. Despite the fact that she and I were careful to not show any displays of affection in front of the guys on the tier, she erred and hugged me for a few seconds before I relented and hugged her back.

I simply told the guys that I was being moved and that the hug was merely a sisterly hug. I immediately processed this anguish and placed it with all of the rest. I, in my insanity, envisioned marriage with this woman as being a high point in my wretched existence, but being forced to view a cell on one-E without Ms. Parker hurt. Plus, it had changed (for the worse) since a V.L. "chief" was down there because he had been stabbed up by the folks, he was extra antagonistic towards the folks (and ex-folks). Ms. Parker would sneak down to see me, but I had to show her that in so doing she was potentially going to arouse suspicions, so she'd then begin to write me under a pseudonym for awhile. But I knew that "all good things don't last."

Chapter 5: The Wild Ones

My cellmate on 1-E and I got along real well, but since he was a V.L. he was ordered to move to the top gallery with all of the V.L.s in an attempt to separate; when you separate from someone it makes it easier to hate them. I hated that they didn't see beyond the gang affiliations; there was an actual war being waged on us and here we sat waging it on each other. This solidified our loss. I was hurt that they couldn't see that we were all basically the same, minus different gang affiliations (or in my case, past affiliations). We were villified by the system simply because of our heritage and environment; our destruction was seemingly visible at conception. We walked right into it. We had no "inalienable rights" like the rest of America's citizens; in fact, we were treated like illegal aliens and our incarceration was the deportation most illegal aliens fear. I guess the only "right" we had was to be bogusly arrested.

Though I had been removed from the folks for over a year, they still tried to relegate me as an associate of them. My cellmate played a role in quashing that thought. Though I was trying to follow Christ, the retaliatory mindset that I had been raised with did try to rear its head again telling me that I should celebrate the fact that someone stabbed him up. I used to ask my cellmate, "House", why was he still involved with those guys considering that he didn't have the same respect for them as he did when he was younger (he was only 22 years old then). He didn't answer, but simply shrugged his shoulder as if the "I don't know" wasn't readily visible from that response. I constantly saw guys stay aligned to their gangs out of a fear, or a misplaced loyalty. The tension on the tier resulted in no less than 3 riots.

Sadly, this animosity wasn't simply for that tier because all around the jail there seemed to be so much tension; a riot was happening every day. I would learn that my guy from 103rd, DeSean would get his vengeance on the school wing on the V.L. he said he hated. He stabbed him in the stomach a few times resulting in a colonoscopy bag for the victim. I hated to hear that, but I was glad that the guy didn't die; nor was DeSean charged (I too was shocked). It seemed that the same genocide that we participated in prior to our incarceration, we were bent on finishing it while we languished in jail. The sheer frivolity of the perceived infractions pained me, but it did cause for me to be more thankful to God that I was no longer a part of the genocide.

The love I had begin to nurture and appreciate life (of others because my own was something else) felt good to have, but I really hurt seeing guys like me unconscious as to the seriousness of life. The mental depravity we suffered seemed to negate our ability to love one another without Christ. I was conscious that I would be in the same situation as they were in. But I wasn't the only one to have grown tired of the incessant rioting over the jail; so too would the administration. They begin to call in their S.O.R.T (Special Operation Response Team) to agitate guys, though they posited that it was to bring "order" to the jail. I wondered how could chaos become organized simply because prison is essentially a dystopia. Plus, these guards in their billy clubs, shields, helmets, and barking dogs would never be an effective "peacemaking" policy.

They'd wake us up at 7:00 a.m. yelling for us to get to the day- room and sit (for hours) with our hands on the wall as they searched for items they knew they'd never find, or if they found them, they'd know they'd never stop them from coming inside of the prison anyway. God forbid they had to make an "example" out of someone because they had the hatred to make the Rodney King beating look like a game of tag played by children. Other times they'd hit guys simply because they could get away with it. I don't know if I could accurately describe the dehumanization, especially since incarceration by its very nature is dehumanizing. The way the c/o's deal with us; the way the courts treat us; the way society perceived us only compounded that. It effectively emasculates guys who were so proud at one point, but pride is easily mitigated when we don't have the weapons to force respect. I found it odd because many had killed for less worse treatment than these activities done by the S.O.R.T team.

It seemed that the only thing to have quelled the violence was the influx of drugs that came in after. I don't know if the administration intentionally let them in in order to quell the violence, but I know that it seemed smart. Whatever it was, it accomplished what a million guards couldn't do: brought false peace. I guess everybody was too high or getting too much money to allow for gang culture to effect how they did their time. We all knew that in order to maximize profit, there had to be some unity amongst the gangs. If there is nothing else certain, all gangs have a desire to make money so any friction between them was silenced for economic purposes; it was good for business and the fact that it didn't yield bloodshed was merely collateral.

Even the wilder gangbangers were often forced to concede to those in authority for the sake of the gang. It was odd for me to see so many guys in their drug filled haze, as if they didn't have a beast to contend with called the judicial system. It was nice, only because I was still in contact with Ms. Parker. I knew that her child's dad was in jail, and if I were smarter, I would have wondered if she didn't have a visible pattern. I would eventually get smarter.

I figured that since I was ''new'' to her I was to be held dear (at least in my mind). But upon seeing an old classmate from the school wing begin to tell me what was transpiring on the school wing. As I was told, basically, that I had been replaced, so in true childish fashion, I questioned her about this. She had come to the tier and I asked her about it. I couldn't tell if it was guilt, shame, or both because she looked odd. In my defense, my dealings with females prior to my incarceration was merely 14-19 year old girls, but with most of those dealings I was in control because I didn't care for them more than they cared for me. Plus, I wasn't incarcerated so I wasn't a dependant. This woman, 16 years my senior had my mind every way, but up. I used to be able to pride myself on being indifferent to females, because I knew we only hurt when we care. I wished to God that I didn't care.

I begin to question my decision as soon as I did it; I regretted not simply appreciating what we had (at one point) and learned that just like seasons, relationships change. I guess that my love for her was so great that I couldn't fathom the reality that I may have been merely one in a long line of incarcerated lovers. I suppose the psychopathy that I had diagnosed myself with was viable because I seemed to have forgotten of the abhorrent circumstance that I was in and focused on my broken, weak heart. I wanted to doubt her confessed love for me, but I felt it was pointless and that since I had so few victories I may as well as accept her feelings as genuine.

She truly drove me crazy, but this insanity brought me to a reality that I needed to be re-introduced to. I had long known that the person who cared the least in a relationship had the most power; clearly I was powerless because I loved her more than life itself; granted, I never loved my life; I never even liked it. I was glad that she did make contact with me a few months after our last conversation telling me, "I can't stand seeing you and others go through this." I guess she saw me as some type of wounded animal and she tried to remove the "splinter" from my proverbial paw like I was a wounded animal; on some levels she did.

I tried to distance myself from the pain that I was in, and this was made somewhat easier knowing that I had another court date approaching. The court was trying to decide what it was going to do with an armed robbery charge that transpired on the night of the March 28, 1993 murder (the one in which several liars claimed to have seen me). This robbery was believed to have been committed by the same person; I concur, it surely looked as if it was, but sadly I didn't commit either crime. Though, on many levels, as I contended with a broken heart, I felt like I was in grade school and being dumped by Talisa Mitchell all over again. The only difference between then and when I dealt with Ms. Parker is that during the former I was still innocent in every sense of the word, but as I dealt with the latter, I was tainted by the streets and the only "good" thing was that the heartbreak brought me closer to humanity.

It also brought me closer to the reality that I was on an inescapable journey to prison. A place I had instinctively known that "men didn't change for the better; where imperfect men became bad; where bad men became worse." I wondered what would I ultimately become, but I tried to go under a premise that if I went with God, it wouldn't matter where I went. It seemed that the U.S. had genocidal ambitions; or maybe I had grown paranoid based on my situation. And though my faith in God was real, it didn't offset the anguish because of the life without parole sentence I contended with; I felt as if I were floating in the Atlantic Ocean without a life preserver, yet being circled by sharks hoping to catch me more vulnerable than my circumstance surmised; it made every breath feel as if the sting of death approached; I lived in the shadows of it, but was incapable of ever crossing over into an actual existence.

Unbeknownst to me I would be moved because they were planning on transferring me quickly after they decided to drop the charge. May be they figured that charge was like squeezing "blood from a turnip." I was glad that there were a few brothers on the tier with whom I had a deep spiritual relationship due to their being on the school wing at one time in their county jail stint. With their help, I was trying to strengthen my spirit to get ready for prison.

My brother's Carlos and Chris had given me words of encouragement, telling me to "go in the power of Christ", but I felt only weakness. I did look forward to developing it however. I was also going to miss many of the brothers in whom I could trust; plus after 5 years in the Cook County jail, 1 was tired of it. As I was being transferred, they brought Tony down there with me because we both had seemingly Greek alphabets as prison sentences. We were separated from all of the other transfers. As we talked, I silently asked myself, "How did I end up ending up with a natural life sentence?"

Another World

I hated that I was treated like Hannibal Lector upon transport to prison. The shackles from my hands to my waist; from my waist to my ankles with only a mask missing. As I watched cars driving pass, it became clear that the system thought that I didn't deserve any more moments outside of a prison cell. But internally, and with every fiber of my being I resisted that thought; the present reality was lending credence to that notion. Though the bus ride took about 90 minutes, it seemed like an eternity I was given to ponder the hand before me. The bus ride was comparable to the guilty verdicts, yet it seemed to have more hopelessness with it.

My cellmate received 32 years for killing his girlfriend. Well, actually he was fighting some guys and she jumped in to help, but she had a weak heart and died so they charged him with her murder.

As outlandish as this sounds, anyone familiar with the judicial system can attest to plenty more miscarriages of "justice", especially to African descended people. The judicial abuses of power is the only thing consistent within the system.

The required attire was blue jumpsuits and cheerleading shoes, prisoners called "Marsha Brady's" because if you've ever seen the show *Brady Bunch*, their identical. The main issue with those shoes was that they were so thin that if you stepped on a roach you would feel it as if you had no socks on. Prison had the capability to equalize its inhabitants (even if only in miniscule ways), but the orientation phase of it placed you all on the same footing because no matter what you had prior to prison, orientation didn't allow for you to reap the benefits from it. It was compounded by seeing guards carrying machine guns and rifles, but I was unarmed and unable to defend myself; for all intents and purposes I was a sitting duck.

It was during this time that my "godmother" and "god sister" had re-planted themselves in my life. I was glad to have heard from them, especially since my god mother had battled with cocaine addiction. When I first received a letter from them I immediately began to think of our times going to carnivals; of our times of playing Nintendo (video game from the 80's); and having water gun fights. There never was any shortage of fun at their house, and since my god sister was an only child, they loved our presence. The only negative to her (as a kid) was everyone knowing that she had a drug problem, and though it bothered us, she seemed able to function well enough, which in turn normalized addiction (at least in my view). In our neighborhood every other person seemed bound by something; be it crack, alcohol, or even bound by violence, everyone was addicted.

I had noticed that she always had a sad expression during her times visiting me; she told me that I was always "the sweetest little boy" and that she couldn't believe I was in jail. I told her I was sorry that I turned "sour", but I also told her I didn't know when it happened because it seemed to have come in increments. I felt more guilt over having let another person down by my placement in prison.

My attempts at sleep were futile for the first few nights because the guards would check the integrity of the bars every night at 11:00 p.m. by tapping (banging) a steel bar against them making a loud clanging sound. Though I've never been able to adjust to that, it has become less of a hindrance to my troubled sleeping patterns. The next day I saw an old cellmate from the county jail working in the kitchen, and it was good to see him, but sadly it was inside of a prison. He too had the perpetual look of misery that I had thought I monopolized. I posit that if you don't have that look, or something close to it, then there is the possibility that you enjoy it.

Gino and I talked often when I went out for meals; he told me that all of our friends from the school wing had passed through. He and I were real close at one point of my incarceration, but I begin to gravitate towards God while he stayed linked to the folks. I noticed that the dynamic of our relationship had shifted from "buddies" to mere associates. During this time in this receiving prison, I often wondered where Tony and I would be sent to; on my fourth day there my calculation sheet (document with prison sentence) came and it removed any concerns as to where I would be going, but as to was it going to transpire as the courts wished. My first thought was to turn it into confetti, but I decided it would be used as a testimony of God's power.

The purpose of receiving was to transition guys from county living to prison existence; you were unable to buy anything while there; you weren't allowed visits, leaving you totally reliant on the state. It was a difficult phase because I grew used to seeing loved ones.

This exacerbated an already hard situation. The gravity of my situation seemed more tangible, as if sitting inside of a dungeon didn't.

I had been praying to God to allow Tony and me to go to Stateville prison, as opposed to Menard, which was about 5 hours from Chicago. I figured that God owed me AT LEAST that for allowing this injustice to occur. I would eventually learn that "Snakeville" was a better title, and for the same reason I considered State's Attorneys "Snakes Attorneys"; it was due to their willingness to use whatever means to convict; perjury and planted evidence was acceptable. And since prison was merely a microcosm of the judicial system, it fit perfectly.

I really didn't rest well (even contemporaneously), but I felt that it had to do with the nature of my incarceration, and not simply my incarceration. The odd dreams that I was tormented by didn't help either. My most vivid one was one involving a guy, about 7'0 feet tall; he had snatched a kid from off of my mother's block. I saw it and went and got my brother Steven and a Glock 9 millimeter and a .380 Sig Sauer to hunt for this giant, we entered a house, but found an *X-Files* character, "Fox Mulder" who was also looking for the child. We then heard that the giant had kidnapped my godsister, but we found her, but were unable to locate the boy. We shot the giant upon seeing him leave another house, but our bullets were ineffective. The giant then carjacked someone, but as we shot him in the car, our bullets worked and we "slayed the giant".

I don't have the proper schooling to properly psychoanalyze the meaning of this dream, but throughout the course of this dream I kept "feeling" as if I was the "giant" in need of eradicating. There were too many subtle hints that this giant was me, but I also posited it may have meant Tony was the giant in need of destruction. But I guess until Sigmund Freud returns from the grave, the meaning behind this dream will remain a mystery.

It was because of dreams like that that I had started keeping a journal in the first place, Plus Oscar and mom had told me long ago that I should keep one for the purpose of using words for empowerment not violence. I couldn't have imagined that this would be the catalyst for my love of writing to have been re-invigorated.

Me and Tony had been able to meet at a church service while we still were in Joliet. He accepted Christ as the altar call was made, and I was glad because I got tired of him often in trouble with the staff in the cook county jail. He had spent years in "S.I." (Secured inmates); a unit for "troublemakers" in the county jail. He had several altercations with the guards and the culmination was him assaulting some with a broom. I commended him on his choice and he said, "I'm tired of thinking and being how I am; I know it's gone take God to change me." That is the realization of mostly all who accept Christ, but most don't realize that it's not simply a one moment decision; it's an everyday one.

Another negative attribute of Joliet is that since orientation doesn't allow for you to buy TV's, or radio's, all you hear all day is guys re-living war stories, whore stories and every other kind imaginable. I hated this because these subconscious thoughts were being planted, and I had no control over them, so it would implant secular and sinful content into my dreams. I had basically been so used to tormenting dreams that it seemed natural; as sad as that seems. It's just sad that the dehumanization, depression and lack of peace are deemed acceptable.

It had only been 7 days since I had last been on a visit, because at this point my family was still diligent, so this deprivation was missed when it occurred. I hated that it took this ordeal to make me realize how loved I actually was. But the confirmation of us getting to "Snakeville" was a pleasantry we couldn't fail to consider, we were on the way to really start our prison sentence, but this in no way implied conceding to it. At least not for me because to do so would mean conceding to the gates of hell; this hell didn't generate heat from it, but depravity and loneliness with its flames called prison bars.

The processing was similar to Joliet's, but it was nothing because Tony and I had finally become cellmates. We had no choice but to ponder how we were where we were. Though my sister Nicole had made it known to him how much she hated for him to hang out with me, we both disregarded that. I guess this justifies her hatred at him for not listening to her. Sometimes I hate him too. I knew I had some culpability in dismissing her desires, but at the end of the day how responsible or rational do we expect 16 year olds to be? I'd rap the 2Pac songs from memory and we'd recall a lot of the negativity that we had to surpass while growing up and it's crux was our current position.

We'd only been cellmates for a couple of days before they decided that since we both had red identification cards that we couldn't be in the same cell together, implications of us being "escape risks".

I suppose anyone with Greek alphabets for a prison sentence is an "escape risk", but they didn't see that. I was able to early on assess the administration's rationale as being, flawed at best. They were the smartest dumb people I had ever had the misfortune of meeting.

Snakeville University

It was a class reunion, of sorts. I mean, if you ever find yourself wondering where someone is when you haven't seen them in awhile; odds are they were in prison (at least in a urban community setting). I found it ironic that more of us seemed to have been in prison, as opposed to in school. I didn't get a good chance to really speak with them (then) but it would be plenty of chances to do so (unfortunately). It bothered me how much of our youth and potential was being wasted. This the nature of the beast.

My next cellmate after Tony was a cool guy and he was my age, but he was moronic. He did, however, concede with me that prison can teach us things about life that no school ever could; at the least how we should appreciate it. As much as I liked him, he was depressing to be around.

He was scheduled to go home in a few months, but he stayed in segregation causing for his outdate to continually be postponed. His disdain for officers was the main cause for him to lose his "good time" (reduced sentence for good behavior). He told me when I asked him why couldn't he just 'chill out and go home?' to be with his family, he simply shrugged his shoulders and said, "I can't let nobody disrespect me." I understood that peculiar outlook, but that was too vague, but I didn't inquire any further. I too had animus for those in power, simply because too often they operated as if they were above the laws they were supposed to uphold.

I had asked him one day what was his intentions once he was released, and no matter how disappointed I was to hear his reply, I wasn't surprised. I always asked soon to be released guys what were their plans, as if to live vicariously through them, but he simply wanted to go back to selling drugs. I was aware that despite society believing that prisons are full of murderers and rapists, the prison population expanded because of drug sentencing becoming the norm. I was trying to help him see that his thoughts determined his life, not his circumstances. I was told that my optimism was an unfamiliar road to travel and that he couldn't because he had to stick to what he knew. I guess everyone sticks to "what they knew".

I must admit that this orientation was pivotal in my spiritual growth; I suppose because of the silence that I was fortunate enough to have been given. But ultimately, my silence would soon be crowded out by the noise of general population as I made my way to its walls on December 10, 1998. My next cellmate was a 43 year old ex-gang brother of mine. He had been gone over 20 years; hearing numbers like that made me cringe, but I was convinced that God would "do the right thing" so I would never see numbers like that (clearly God and I had different definitions on "right"). The age difference notwithstanding, but he and I agreed that the gang that we grew up in had, loved at one point, it clearly wasn't the same.

There is something more ominous about prison than the county jail, I suppose that this was why my mom, upon seeing me the next day cried. She told me that she sent me about $600.00 for me to buy some things (TV, radio, clothes etc.) to at least make life a bit more tolerable. This ate me up because I've always prided myself on taking care of myself before I was incarcerated, even being so young, I was able to give siblings money if they asked , but now I was a dependent; and I didn't like it.

Unbeknownst to me, this would be my first and last visit at Snakeville (for a couple of years). I had been called for a writ the next day, but I was under the mistaken impression that this writ was for the hospital and not court. I had no idea I'd be leaving so quickly, but I knew that my case had been reversed even before I left the county jail, and I still couldn't fathom going back so quickly. The Appellate court had reversed my conviction months prior stating that the police erred in refusing me my pain medication for the broken jaw and for not allowing my mom to see me, whereas I was a juvenile: that's illegal. But when has something being illegal for them ever stopped them?

Let's Do It Again

I had the misfortune of failing to take any of my legal work with me because of my erroneous belief that I was going to the hospital, so I left all of my pertinent paper work in prison. In my ride to the court house, the thought was that I would be in for even more of a difficult battle because of that fact. I was somewhat overwhelmed by that, plus the c/o's told me that some guy my age (22) had killed himself just days ago; why they felt the need to tell me, I don't know, but I suppose after they saw my age they were just making conversation. Hell of a conversation starter.

I told them that Caucasian's were more prone to kill themselves than African American's, due to (from my) belief that since we have had such hard lives for all of our lives this creates a familiarity with pain, so we're more capable to deal with it. This kid had only a few months before he went home. I must admit, I contemplated suicide pre and post incarceration, but all I could see that stopped me was my visualizing my mother and more pain that caused her.

He chose to relinquish life, while I was going to be fighting for mine… literally. I would have to fight the same racist community, plus now they had even more animosity because I was given a re-trial. The looks on their faces showed me that they would have preferred to just grab the noose and gasoline and be done with it.

I had been assigned to Judge Lewinsky (who I learned they called him "no win Lewinsky"). He had denied me the chance to return to the prison to gather my legal material; it was well in his power to have granted it. I surmised that this was a clear indication of just how he felt about my situation; and this victim being a Caucasian was probably the main reason. The Snakeville Officer's who had drove me to the court house were now obligated to leave me to the custody of the county deputies, who would in turn make sure I was returned to the county jail; The same county jail that I had just spent 5 years at.

My waiting to go back to the county jail was further aggravated, by county jail inmates wanting to know what Snakeville was like, as if I had just returned from Disneyland. I told them that it was a nice place to visit, but they wouldn't want to live there.

I was being my usual sarcastic self, but there was a great deal of truth to that comment. I suppose that their reasons varied for being curious; some from fear, because Snakeville became notorious only a couple of years before. It was a violent and depraved place, and the inmates did control it, but that all changed once convicted killer Richard Speck was seen on a video in female under wear, getting high and basically having the time of his life. Oprah Winfrey had got a hold of said tape, which forced the prisons to take back control of the prisons in 1996.

Upon returning to the county, the only fortune I had was that in receiving I wasn't processed as the guys newly arriving were.

The dehumanization of the strip search; the bending and coughing etc. was a ritual that I didn't care if I never endured again (I would endure it again). They placed me in a special "Hannibal Lecter" type cage secluded from everyone else since I was a prison inmate technically. I was going to be sent back to division 9, and I was relieved because I knew most of the staff and inmates there because I had spent over 5 years there less than a month prior.

The first person I saw was a Lt. Clemmons (an individual with whom I had a amiable relationship), he said, "who yo' lawyer to have gotten you back so fast?" I told him that my case was reversed prior to my leaving, so this was why it seemed as if I received preferential treatment. He just smirked as if to say, "Yeah, right."

I had been placed on my old school wing (2-H) but it was no longer a school wing, but a wing specifically for the housing of individuals from prison. I erroneously presumed that the guys from prison would have more intelligence than the school wing inhabitants; I was sadly mistaken. The first thing a guy asked was, "What you is?" (What gang am I in). I told him that I was a Christian, and his lip turned up as if he drank a 3 month old milk. It struck me how much disdain he had at my beliefs, but it made no difference to me. I was placed in the first cell on the gallery (deck) and was by myself because the old VL in there opted to move in with his gang brother. I saw that Officer Lewis (same Lewis the folks thought tried to set them up) was working the tier; he came to the cell and asked me was I cool (meaning was I alright).

This was prompted because as he saw me I had my head in my hands, but I merely was trying to rest and prepare for another round at the gauntlet; I told him I was and he left.

I asked Lewis to call Chaplain Baird and to let him know that I was back in division 9. I liked Chaplain Baird because he was a genuine believer. He'd himself been in trouble with the law as a youngster, but God allowed for him to find Him, so he felt it was his duty to try to mentor others as he had once been. This is a true mark of a Christian. I was his assistant prior to leaving, so I felt I should speak with him. Plus, he'd allow me to use the phone so that my family didn't have to pay for the calls after I had completed my tasks of organizing closets; grading test scores and all of the "grunt work" entailed with being an

Assistant.

He immediately came and took me to his office and began asking me how I was doing, and how was Stateville. I told him that I witnessed a spirit of "gloom" lingering over the prison, but the sad thing is that I understood why or how it was there. I told him that if walls could talk, I'm sure they'd forever scream like a banshee in a guttural sound of anguish. He laughed, but he knew I was mostly serious in that assessment. He'd been in a medium security, but it would almost seem guaranteed that the misery of prison extends to maximum and medium prisons.

Before I could finish, he'd immediately had me started right back where I left off at grading papers since he'd not replaced me after I left a month ago. He also didn't do what the majority of people do who aren't incarcerated do, look down on us and relegate us all to idiot status. There is always an indication of true brotherhood by the sacrifices we make for each other, and our willingness to listen to our brother.

After spending a few hours with the Chaplain, I was sent back to the tier with some cosmetics from him since I was very much still on the "new" and guys didn't like it because they didn't understand the fact that I had been in that building for over 5 years, so I should have had the favor that I did. Then the Christian brothers introduced themselves to me they also gave me a couple of things the Chaplain didn't have until we went to the store.

We would go through a multitude of "lock downs" (restrictions) for any number of reasons, but the oddity of it was a lot of it was due to the insanity displayed by the old fools on the writ tier that I was on. During this time my, then, cellmate Larry was trying to help me with my legal work. I guess the fire eventually would have had to grow in me. He attempted to help, but his incompetence only made things worse, but sadly I didn't realize this until after the damage was done. It truly was a hard learning process. And no sooner than that occurred, the gangs had decided to separate by tiers; the brothers to the top tier and the folks to the bottom. I was housed with another non gang member, with whom I found quite a bit of solidarity.

I was in the cell with Sanchez for only a few months before I had to move to make room for the folks they wanted in that cell.

I must admit that I did NOT like feeling like I was subjected to the whims of the idiots; my pride really was being eradicated, which is what all Christian's need, but that didn't make it any easier to deal with.

Chapter 6: Men Of God

I was placed in the cell with a guy named Geral Earl whose co-defendant was in division 10 with me: "Fuss". We'd both been incarcerated at about the same time, but he was still part of his gang, but that didn't deter me from giving him the benefit of the doubt. Another brother over there, Cornelius, was also involved in his gang, but I was influential because we knew a lot of the same people from the streets, plus he was seeking God and I was trying to help him find him.

Cornelius and I had grown closer through his attendance at the Bible Study that I conducted on the tier four times a week. He and I knew a lot of the same people, so this was a catalyst for our bond to strengthen; though our ties were based upon my gang banging days. We spent probably more time than we should have, talking on our misspent youth, but we were trying to rectify it by following Christ. I personally feel that the only way to be of any lasting good would be if I allowed for Christ's person to be lived through me. Since He gave His life for me, I felt that I had *TO LEARN TO TRUST HIM* with mine. My living, and decisions, pre Christ, were catastrophic, so I had to be receptive to His guidance. I only now realized that people can't alter the mistakes from their past, but we can transcend and learn from them. This isn't just advice that spiritual people should follow, but anyone weighed down by their past. No sooner than we had grown "comfortable" on the tier that we were on, the staff moved about 12 guys from 2-H to 2-F, for no apparent reason. We had the pleasure of meeting a brother who was going to become instrumental in my spiritual growth.

I was returning from a Bible Study class one night at about 9:30 p.m. and was introduced to Derrick. The first thing that hit me was his deep Tennessee drawl, which always humored me. He looked like he should have been on a college campus, and not fighting the murders that he was fighting. He and I immediately grew close.

It was nice to not have to deal with the manipulative people that 1 had grown accustomed to being around. I had a new trial pending, so I was in need of building my spirit man up and there was no better way to do this than to be surrounded by strong brothers in Christ. I felt that any relief that I would receive would be predicated on my being a "super Christian".

We had fellowship on a daily basis, and no longer did I simply conduct the Bible Study, but other brothers were given a chance to show what God had revealed to them. I felt like a proud father seeing my 'students" growing up in Christ. Since prison was such a dismal place, we felt it necessary for us to grow, so we'd have to at least meet and talk daily. True, no one wants complication in their lives, but the true essence of growth comes from turmoil at least this is how I saw it. Without growth, it's only stagnation to look forward to. And on more than one occasion our fellowship was interfered with by the S.O.R.T (Special operations Response Team) making their presence known.

The proximity of the jail to the city and the greed of the guards made the drug trade flourish inside of the jail, which in turn often times ended with the S.O.R.T team attacking us. On one particular night in 1999, they woke guys up violently. There had been a constant influx of drugs and stabbings throughout the building, so I surmise that the Superintendant wanted to make examples of people. I, to this day, don't understand how can one believe that violence will curtail violence-it only exacerbates it. I had encountered S.O.R.T. often in my time incarcerated, but I had never been touched by them...until this night. I was merely poked in the ribs with a billy club and told to hurry up, but since I noticed they poked everybody, I wasn't as upset after.

This fiasco ended with about a dozen lawsuits against the jail with them all being settled out of court, but with all suits against prisons and jails, since it's the taxpayers money, they can care less. This didn't deter my spiritual growth, even in my legal knowledge, I hated that I only got REALLY serious after my convictions. Then one of my ex-gang "chiefs" came to the tier. Myke had dropped his flags as well, also in an effort to draw near to God. Though he had rank for the mob, our bonds exceeded that. This was because the B.D.'s had told me and a couple of the folks to violate him, but since I knew that it was bogus, I didn't let them do so, and even told them that we were on Myke's side of the conflict.

It was one individual in the gang who wanted Myke violated because Myke didn't send him any money and we all knew Myke had plenty of it. On some levels, since Myke was about 15 years older than me, he almost became like an uncle. I played a role in his sincere desire to draw close to God and away from the gang. I had respected him for that because he had been in the gang for years, and I had less than a decade gangbanging. Our comfortability comes with our familiarity to whatever we're dealing with, and the more comfortable you are is based on how familiar you are. Myke would also be the reason that I was the Chaplains assistant; he was there first and recommended me to the Chaplain.

I was his assistant after Myke had bonded out for his murder charge, and we had been so close that he constantly sent me money because of that. He was genuinely a good guy, just caught up in the streets as all of us potentially were. He had legitimate businesses, as well as the not so legitimate kind. I give him credit because he stayed in touch with me, but he wasn't able to enjoy it for long because he was re-arrested about a year later because of his conflict with the neighborhood police. He would eventually be convicted of his murder, as seemingly everyone was.

Myke had been on the tier with me on 2-F for about 2 months and I noticed his subtle activity within the gang again. I pulled him aside and asked him, "Why are you messing around with them dudes again?" He tried to rationalize it by claiming that he was trying to guide them since they clearly were in need of it. He said he was going to try to bring them peace before someone else was killed in the jail; the stabbings eventually lead to a murder. I told him that I agreed that they needed guidance, but as a Christian, it wasn't his function to realign himself with those dudes who we fought to get away from. I also told him that to bring peace to a demonic based entity was virtually impossible. He shrugged it off, so I decided we should discuss other topics, because as much as I hated his stubbornness, he was still and always will be my brother.

I knew that God challenges us all with the adversarial situations and people that he allows to come into our lives, but that doesn't make the particular situation feel any better, from an emotional standpoint. One day before my second trial for the Bridgeview case, (August 28, 2000)

Myke was stabbed in his effort to attain "peace".

He was talking to a V.L. "chief" who decided he wasn't trying to hear anything about peace. However, it was more of a scratch than a stab wound, because Myke had some semi-professional boxing training, so this mitigated any serious damage; plus he was about 6'3 and 200 plus pounds. Though this could be looked at from a human position, all of his training and size wasn't the ultimate factor on it not being fatal: God's mercy was. I knew that God was watching over him even after he fell back in with the B.D.'s, which opened the door for Satan.

Trial By Fire

I woke up for court at about 3 A.M., since they come to get us at about 4. Yet after they retrieve you, you'll merely be waiting inside of a "bullpen" (cage too small for all its occupants) for hours. I didn't eat because I was fasting in an attempt to garner as much extra favor with God as I possibly could've. I must admit I wasn't expecting the trial to be as it was. My co-defendant Jackson had already been acquitted in 1995, yet the Judge Brownsfield had allowed the prosecution to subpoena him as a witness. The Judge allowed the prosecution to compel (force) his testimony, despite the fact we had a severance of trials.

I was under the mistaken impression that "the justice" this country propagated was attainable, but this was lost after my trial in 1995 and I have long since been justifiably critical of the courts.

I believed that we were guilty until proven innocent; this is what they demonstrated systematically. "The presumption of innocence is now a legal myth." U.S. v Crary, 846 F.Supp.768, 1796-97 (E.D. MO.1994, Judge Clyde Cahill). Even Lawyer Michelle Alexander had discovered YEARS after the fact, that the nature of the criminal justice system has changed. It is no longer concerned with prevention and punishment of crime, but rather with the management and control of the dispossessed."(*The New Jim Crow: Mass Incarceration in the Age of Colorblindedness*. pg 183.) I felt that plenty of cases that I had seen, my own included, had validated that premise. So despite receiving a new trial, I was forever guilty to the predominantly Caucasian community of Bridgeview.

The public defender was of no assistance, since he kept trying to get me to take a 25 year plea deal the state had offered me. In hindsight, I often question why didn't I accept it, but I trusted God for deliverance; wrong or right. They used an alleged statement of Jackson, but that didn't implicate me in any criminal activity, but that's irrelevant because the newspapers had already vilified me as a 16 year old incorrigible human being. At 16 they relegated me as such. I felt the trial was merely semantics; a show to fool the blind that there is "democracy at work". The court's have long gone for convictions, not necessarily truth.

A peer filled jury is almost as fictitious as the justice concept; at least from a "minorities" position. The more disturbing fact is not that out of about 100 potential jurors only about 4 or 5 were Latino or 'African-American', but the oddity was that the state used its challenges to exclude them for seemingly no other reason than their heritage, (this practice is technically illegal).

The end result left me with 10 of 12 Caucasian jurors. I hope my position isn't viewed as cynical, but it's justifiably a view even if it were to be deemed as such.

I can only report the reality as I experienced it and how it was demonstrated throughout my proceedings. The judicial system is even harsher on individuals of my heritage when the victim is Caucasian. The jurors subconsciously viewed me as more violent and less human-than they are. I was conscious that it wasn't "intentional" prejudice, but ingrained and detrimental nonetheless. The images they see reported on the news would lead one to believe that, but anything purposely shown to create the bias will succeed if it's done efficiently enough: it was (is). I tried not to hold it against them because of what they had been exposed to. I knew that as long as we were kept culturally and psychologically severed, it would make it easy to be indifferent to one another's plight.

I constantly had been brought back to my first murder trial; the jury had SIGNIFICANT instances of perjury from the "witnesses"; the jury had verifiable substantial discrepancies between me and the killer; the jury had exonerating forensic evidence, but I was still convicted based upon what they thought about me as a part of a certain demographic only known for gang banging and drug dealing. I fought (still) a continual battle to not be embittered by the treatment the system gave, but it's difficult. I take solace in the fact that no battle worth fighting is not, at least, worth risking a few rounds, sadly, it seemed that I was constantly on the mat.

I often asked God why did He allow me to escape death in the street? Did He do it just to torture me like some omnipotent sadist? It was like these convictions for murder were like psychological hand grenades, dispersing emotional shrapnel throughout my body, but there would e no sweet release of death; there would be nothing but a psychological purgatory forcing me to endure the hell of an unjust conviction and (at best) a questionable conviction. After I returned to the tier this August 30, 2000, my guy asked, "What they do?" I simply shook my head "no" implying a guilty verdict; no one else asked me anything that night. I began to wonder why did I trust God because He seemingly didn't concern Himself with me. I felt He was just like my biological dad.

My brother Derric told me that, "There must be some things that God wants to purge from you Marcos." I asked him why would it need to be so painful, but he, nor I, was able to answer that. I always believed that God was the cause of all, if not most, of my pains since if He allowed it, then He too was culpable. I had been sentenced a few months later and the judge wasted no time in sending me back to prison- even though I had another court date in front of him. I was glad that I didn't stay at the receiving prison (Joliet) for too long.

I remained faithful, even while dejected by the circumstance that continued to haunt me: incarceration. This created anger in me towards God; I did still love Him. I hated that I allowed for a negative disposition to dictate my feelings. I was even more upset as guys would offer me the cliche, "Let go and let God" spiel, as if that fit every situation. As I thought about my trial, I would not have known that my proceedings would have been something out of a Perry Mason movie. As Derric, took the stand, the D.A. asked him about the alleged signed statement he signed, but he kept saying that he "didn't recall" the statement or "vaguely" recalled it. Even had he conceded to it, it wasn't inculpatory towards me, it only stated that I was present, and as

DOZENS of Illinois cases posit mere presence at a crime scene doesn't make an individual accountable for the actions of others.

I strongly believed that the adverse circumstances that I was going through would expose any false motives or ulterior motives that I may have had regarding my sincerity with God. I constantly wrestle(d) with that, and though I welcome the exposure of any false pretenses, I most certainly wanted the persistent, continual and constant anguish that I was in to stop, but I knew that it would NEVER stop as long as I was incarcerated unjustly. And since I didn't have the luxury to believe in "luck", I had to gauge life by cause and effect. It dawned on me that my criminality was a cause and my imprisonment was the effect of a plethora of wrong choices.

I re-entered "Snakeville" on November 16, 2000, just in time to spend my 24th birthday in prison. Lucky me. There would be no birthday cakes; there would be no ice cream, but merely barbed wires and steel bars to go with the gift that keeps on taking: natural life prison sentence.

The cellmate I received in orientation was set to go home later that week. I had a tendency to ask guys with whom I was cool their plans upon release, I suppose to see if has the incarceration taught them anything beneficial. He at least had good intentions, but we've all heard that the road to hell was paved with those. I don't know if he ever did keep them, but I know my cellmate after him wasn't even going to try. He unapologetically told me that he had every intention to go right back to the corner to sell drugs. I was upset with him for not listening (he was only 18), plus at the end of the day, I was just as ignorant, if not more so at one point in my life. I suppose it takes life altering scenario's to cause .for people to at least think differently.

He used to tell me he didn't know if he could do the time I had been given, but I told him that "If you have the sentence, you will fight it, kill yourself or you will do it." Plus, I didn't plan on doing it anyway. The Bible said, "Nothing is secret that shall not be made manifest, nor anything hid, that shall not be known and come abroad" (Luke 8 v 17). I believe that my innocence will HAVE TO be made known and the elusive "justice" will be attained. Or at the very least, the excessive sentence would be removed once people became aware of it.

I usually didn't let people know that I was given life without parole as a juvenile. I took that sentence as a type of *Scarlet Letter* as Mr. Nathaniel Hawthorne posited in his book of the same title. It was embarrassing to have to face the fact that I never had a chance to live. The woman in the book was ostracized and forced to wear an A on her chest (for adulterer). The JLWOP was my own "scarlet letter" and I hated it.

I was done with orientation after about a week, and the oddity of it was I was "glad" to finally go to population where all of the 'pacifiers' were being sold: TV's, radio's and the like. It didn't take me too long to realize that buying that was costly.

I had come to realize that those devices took guys focus off of the important things, such as working on their case or their minds. I would be mindful to not be so concerned with the TV, but with my legal work, which was somewhat difficult because I felt that the court's didn't listen anyway.

My first cellmate was a brother whom I had known from the county jail. Melvin was a good Christian brother, and I needed that to help me in my spiritual walk; I don't imply that he was perfect but I do posit that there is strength in numbers. I was blessed to have received him as a cellmate, clearly I could've got worst. He had been there (Snakeville) for about 18 months, so he was explaining how things really went; they didn't automatically go how the administration would have us new prisoner's believe. No sooner than I was placed in population, we were placed on a "lock down", which I merely consider a restriction since the prison was locked down anyway. I would come to learn that we would stay on those throughout the course of the years.

One individual assaults an officer and the entire prison was penalized; this was a lot like the accountability theory. I went to court the next day, which made my judge's desire to get rid of me so fast reckless, since he knew that I had to come back to court so soon. Even before I left, the lawyer asked him "why are you sending him back to prison knowing he has another court date?" He just smiled and said," I want him to get started on his prison sentence as soon as possible." It behooves me how anyone can believe that we'll receive justice when those to whom the law gives the power abuse it with such impunity and disdain of those to whom they are supposed to make sure their constitutional rights are protected.

I knew that I could be "difficult" at times, but this judge gave even me a run for my money. He had re-sentenced me to life without parole and added another 15 years; for good measures despite that being illegal. I didn't care about it due to the fact that it was pointless. I was more mentally drained than not, but that was because I strongly believed that God was going to deliver me at that moment. As I returned to "Snakeville", I had no choice but to dwell on the double standard that the system employs. Defense lawyers can be sued for misrepresenting cases, but prosecutor's can't even if they conceal favorable and exculpatory evidence. I was a prime example of the devastation lies can have on an individual's life.

Considering that I was a poor African-American, I was somewhat conscious of the possibility of it, but it didn't negate the pain. There is quantifiable evidence showing the prevalence of wrongful convictions. The Innocence Project and Innocence Network have established eyewitness testimony is often unreliable and that led to 223 people (as of 2008" the numbers have only grown) serving more than 2,500 years collectively in prison before being exonerated. Columbia Law published a study on the first 200 exonerations obtained as a result of post conviction DNA testing; they discovered 158 out of 200 (over 75%) of wrongful convictions are based, in part or completely on mistaken identification. I couldn't compete with such depths of corruption, or injustice.

I had seen my mom and step dad with my niece Tanae, who was 10 at he time, and I was grateful because I hadn't seen them for a couple of weeks. I always worried about them when I didn't see them for an extended period. But, people have a tendency to suddenly disappear when prison's seemingly final aspect comes into play. It seems people resign themselves to this being my existence, so I had to not allow for their perceptions to guide my beliefs. Obviously this was at times hard, considering the system is designed to sever familial bonds and bonds one has with his respective communities; granted often times the ties we have with our communities are found in depraved actions.

I suppose that prison's habit of throwing people into a state of hopelessness due to the "finality of" is understandable on some levels, but from an emotional standpoint it is heartbreaking. Based, upon Donald Bramans, *Doing Time On the Outside*: *Incarceration and Family Life in Urban America* (Ann Arbor: Un. Of Mich. Press 2004) pg. 220, he states, "As relationships between family and friends become strained or false, not only peoples understanding of one another diminished, but because people are social, they themselves are diminished as well." I suppose that this justifies, on some levels, the feelings of abandonment that I was going to have to contend with. I was understanding the system's functions were to, among other things, to divide and sever a prisoners ties with their family and community. It works perfectly.

It was a little prior to the 2000 presidential election that we were placed on restriction because a lieutenant was hit in the head with a weight; for the record he called an individual a bitch, so the prison logic was that he deserved it. Yet, this extra time was the catalyst for me to get serious about following politics. I'd often watch the debates or listen to news reports, but I was skeptical of the media's perception, especially in light of the way they demonized me. I was hopeful that George Bush Jr. wouldn't win, and it seemed that he wasn't going to, but then Florida came under question even after it had been given to democrat Al Gore. I suppose that Mr. Bush having a brother as governor didn't hurt; I believed it helped.

I'm not foolish enough to believe that there is a major difference between democrats and republicans, but I was against Bush for the sheer fact that he had allowed several individuals to be executed while Governor of Texas where there was strong evidence combating their guilt, or all together destroying it. This spoke volumes to what he felt about, at least my people. So long before Kanye West stated that he "didn't care about black people", I long knew he had no love for us. So, in a country that prides itself on "democracy", it does everything in its power to negate that premise.

There are so many hypocritical practices of this "great nation", but it can't really be surprising where this country's forefathers were the ultimate hypocrites: claiming Blacks were less than human, while having sex with their slaves; claiming we were less than men, yet

116

using us to fight their wars and do their labor. My knowledge of this caused much friction between my God and my consciousness of these realities. The way I saw it was that at every step of the criminal process I had been told I had constitutional rights, but this was in theory only because it seems that the only thing that was protected was the unjust conviction the prosecutor procured via perjured testimony and inadequate evidence. This is "the American Way" that I was familiar with. It almost parallels with my not being loved by my father; regardless to what this country thinks about me, I belong to it... unfortunately in nationality only.

My battle for spiritual growth was stunted by the death of my grandmother Amy Norman. She was my mother's mom and though this January 9th 2001 date is one I'll never forget, I was somewhat glad that she had a nice 79 years on this earth. I seemed to be more hurt that she passed away while I was in prison than anything, because it seemed as if prison had taken enough from me already, and I wasn't ready to begin losing loved ones to them as well. I had started reminiscing on the times when my mom would take me to grandma's house in Dayton, Ohio to stay with her and my aunt "Pumpkin". This was done on occasion to get me away from my biological father.

I used to love going to her house, because there was a cute little girl that lived next door about my age with whom I used to play "jacks" for what must have been hours. To those unfamiliar with "jacks", it was a game where there are dozens of steel or plastic shapes ("Jacks") and you had to drop a little ball and before it fell to the ground, see how many "jacks" you were able to pick up. I suppose this is now exposing how ancient I am. At any rate, that little girl wasn't the main reason I enjoyed going to Ohio, but the fact that most of my mom's family stayed down there and they doted over me, which was contrary to how my dad's family who treated me about as equally as he did (indifferently) and on occasion hateful.

Grandma would call me from the house to go to the yard with her to pick greens and tomatoes, "Snapper" come on out here and help grandma baby." (She called me "Snapper" because of a soap opera character played by David Hasselhoff because I had a curly afro as he did.) It seems that I only had happy times in Ohio, whereas I wasn't belittled for always having two of my favorite toys in hand: G.I. Joe action figures Flint and Destro; those were the equivalent of my security blanket like Linus carried around with him on the cartoon/comic strip "Charlie Brown". I know that a mother's love and a grandmother's love are different, but they both have an innate compassion for you that made me at least, feel like the most precious child in the world. This feeling would never last in Chicago.'

I hated that it wasn't enough to translate into my teenage years, where I disregarded the love from people that I knew loved me, and allowed for the disdain I had for myself to be a cause for me to disregard the evils I knew were wrong. This in turn caused for me to become de-sensitized to the evils; they now were deemed right. My self hate was all that I remember, even knowing I was loved by some of my family. These thoughts were all sparked by my grandma's death, and though I may have even shed few tears for it, inside I have never stopped crying. Please note that the lack of tears isn't indicative of just how hurt I was, but that these walls had constructed "walls" within my soul that were (are) difficult to destroy.

My current cellmate, Will, had a gang brother next door to us who dealt in illegal acts while in prison. Since they were gang affiliates, the heat upon him was placed upon our cell as well. This one instance the c/o's came in our cell at about 12a.m. to shake down... or so we premised. Yet, it was more of a ransacking, in my view, than an actual shake down. We made it back to the cell to discover his gang brother wasn't going to be so fortunate.

It is a very disturbing feeling to be awaken from your rest at 12a.m. to being harassed, but I suppose it's better than being awakened only to be put in an eternal sleep. They took his brother to segregation while in house shoes, while it was snowing outside. They do cruel stuff like that simply because they can. They also helped themselves to about $60.00 worth of cigarettes Will was holding for his brother. This, however, was a more common occurrence, where c/o's have (had) a tendency to steal guys cigarettes when the prisons sold them. And most prisoners couldn't complain because they got them from "hustling" anyway, so you couldn't provide a receipt for them. Prison is a place where you learn how to constantly take losses.

It had always been difficult for me to get good rest; this is still true to this day, but after being shook down, it was worse. I was agitated by the sheer disregard for any modicum of rights we believe that we had while in prison, but after the adrenaline rush leaves, existing goes back to what it was- deplorable. Will and I stayed up for about an hour talking about their mistreatment while putting the cell back in order, but finally one of us posited that it was pointless to complain about something that we couldn't alter: it was probably him. I always found it profound that some people who didn't share my Christian views could have more of a "Christian" outlook than I myself had. I was always mindful of my impact on others based upon their perception of me, though I didn't always live righteously.

It wasn't a full two days after the shake down that the c/o' s came to the cell and told Will that he was going to segregation for investigation. Investigation is merely a premise to punish you for not actually having done anything wrong. But this is the environment where guilt by association is as valid as anything in a court of law.

I suppose that life has the same quality. My next cellmate was a guy from Joliet prison. Though it was a receiving prison, it did house general population, but most of them were stigmatized with a reputation of being a "snitch". They closed the prison down and sent a lot of those inmates to various prisons. Though I want to say all of the inmates from Joliet weren't "snitches", I still was leery of anyone from that prison. He was alright and our first few weeks were of no major consequence, whereas we got along primarily because of our communications were on a "mandatory" basis. I mean, I am a recluse by nature. He was a Muslim, so we did have discussions about our faiths, and it wasn't the antagonizing type that I had been a part of sometimes.

The impactful event that altered our relationship was once we were "shook down"(Searched cell) and the c/o.'s found a "stinger". (A make-shift device for boiling water. Insert 2 steel paper clips in the outlet of an extension cord. PLEASE DO NOT HAVE EXTENTION CORD HOOKED UP INTO THE WALL BEFORE INSERTION). In prison, we make do with the materials given. After they found them, however, he didn't accept responsibility for his device so we were sent to segregation this February day in 2002. I was upset with him for that, but I did enjoy the solitude of "seg", whereas it gave me an opportunity to draw nigh to God. The rest of my time would be used for exercising for about 90 minutes, talking with my cellmate and doing legal research. I was fortunate to have been able to file my post conviction petition on May 31, 2001 , so I was having to respond to the State's motions.

On the day of the adjustment committee, I was thinking to myself, "Why am I constantly being forced to answer for things that I didn't do?" First a murder of a guy who I had never seen; segregation for a knife in the county jail and now a "stinger" that didn't belong to me. I grew tired of this false guilt I was being subjected to.

Though he eventually took responsibility for his "stinger", I still kicked out a couple of weeks in "seg" for his actions. I must admit that I seemed to have found some spiritual rejuvenation behind this scenario. I wasn't going to get away unscathed; they gave me 90 days without being able to shop for the claim that my radio wasn't mines; they didn't bother to ask for the contract or receipt that they give us for electronics. I was eventually able to get that corrected after grieving it, but it merely shows just how bogus the system and its extended arm (prison) is.

Chapter 7: Growing Pains

As we were being let out of segregation, I was placed in B-unit and housed with an old V.L. named "Weasel". He was about 45 years old and had been locked up for over 20 years. Despite that, he was cool to talk to, except when he'd begin reminiscing on the depravity of the prison when it was at its apex. He'd made it sound as if it was a nice place to be in; I suppose to some it may have been. He used to tell me that he had just been released from segregation after 2 years, and that he'd probably be on his way back, since he didn't like the atmosphere of the prison, especially since the guys from Joliet prison were down here in Stateville, or as the old timers called it, "the Ville".

His disdain for the c/o's trumped my own, whereas my not liking them wasn't going to make me to do anything to cause any detriment to my legal proceedings, but he seemed to not have any legal proceedings to care about. His disdain would come out in the most frivolous of conversations. I knew that it was going to be hard to try to change the mentality of an individual at least 20 years older than I was, but I had to try. I often told him that if he continued to allow for them to dictate his actions, then that was another dimension of control that he was giving them. He seemed to have accepted that, but I would soon see that it didn't have any lasting impact.

One day a Lt. Wilson was walking pass our cell and he told Weasel, "turn that radio down before I take it." I thought I heard a fire bell ringing because Weasel jumped up and said, "You Ain't Gone Take A Mother®*#!#@# thing from Me!!!" After that outburst "Barney Rubble" (Wilson looked like the cartoon character) left to bring reinforcements; as with most cowardly individuals in authority do; start a fight then run for help. He went and called the tactical team "Orange Crush". They earned their name because of the bright orange jumpsuits they wear. However, they are also are given helmets, vests to protect from being stabbed and billy clubs, along with tear gas guns.

Once the Lt. left, Weasel immediately started packing his property and then threw on his gloves and shoes. NO sooner than he had got his gloves on, the tactical team was at our door. They make it a policy to order the occupants of the cell to go to the rear of it, this is to make their entrance easier into the cell and to see if an individual is going to comply. I went to the back of the cell and though Weasel initially protested, I was able to calm him down and get him to comply. In all honesty, his radio wasn't loud at all; it was just another example of the abuse of power that prisoners are subjected to. I told him, sadly, that it was a no-win situation because when they come, it's no less than 15-20 of them, so it would be pointless, or foolish for them to get bragging' rights for beating him up.

They removed Weasel without incident, but sadly I did come to find out that they beat him up once they got him to "seg", but I guess once they've been called it's hard to tell a dog to sit after you've told them to bite. Wilson's antics would eventually catch up to him; he was hit in the head with a weight for calling someone a bitch. I suppose to some he received a modicum of what he deserved. Sadly, it took my cellmate's going to "seg" for me to really see how detrimental hate of authorities can be; those feelings are never really far removed.

I know how difficult it is to battle lifelong views, especially when the things that we see give credence to our disliking or even hating police, c/o's or anyone in uniform. I had Christ on the inside, yet this didn't remove a lot of the negative feelings that I possessed towards authorities. We tend to be more apt to believe in the things that we've been taught and are comfortable with; usually this is detrimental to our progress.

My next cellmate has indelibly placed himself in my heart, due to his genuine good disposition. He viewed me as an older brother, though it was only by about 3 years, but he had a kind heart and I don't use that description loosely. He was another guy, with whom I believed in his innocence based upon what he told me. I know that society cringes at a prisoner claiming innocent, but over the past decade or so there have been no less than 50 guy's proven innocent, in Illinois alone. Malcolm had only one flaw that I often tried to help him correct: he was always doing everything he could for his gang brothers, I mean to the point of personal detriment.

I told him it would never be enough and that guys would "bleed him dry" if he allowed it. Though he and I weren't cellmates for more than about 6 months, our bond is now one of brotherhood. He and I were separated because the toilet in our cell broke and instead of them fixing it promptly, they figured it was easier to remove us from the cell. It wasn't too much longer after that that the Appellate Court denied my appeal. For the second time they had tried to condemn me for this case to die slowly in prison. I could not rationalize their injustices, because the evidence wasn't so compelling considering the (one of) masterminds stated that I wasn't aware of the crime, but that's irrelevant in the judicial system.

I kept second guessing my choice to go back to trial; all that I heard in my head was the antagonistic deputy saying, "you stuck now, you should've took the 25 years". I wondered how right he may have been. I was comforted with the fact that God was more concerned with His relationship with me and not my comfort; this was good because I can't be "comfortable" in prison.

Though my trust in God was fractured, it wasn't broken. I still did everything in my limited power to try to manifest my vindication; though on some levels, I felt that I didn't deserve it.

I tried to stay preparing for it, even if I didn't get it because I felt it was better than not preparing for it and it appearing.

Though it was worked for, it didn't manifest, yet I wouldn't be deterred.

After Malcolm and I were placed in different cells, he began working at an assignment where the risk of becoming "close" with the female staff was a potential detriment. Not only was he going to work around them, but individuals who may be jealous would work with him as well. This meant that ANY perceived favor he would have received would probably yield negative results because of the fact that some prisoner's despise another simply because they aren't able to incur favor from some female c/o's. The end result would be a transfer to a prison so far down south that it'll be like you've been lost.

On my 26th birthday, I had been told that my brother Myke had been sent to segregation for fighting. I wish I was surprised but I knew Myke had always wrestled with his temper. This only gave me another reason to hate birthdays. I had long since relegated them to holiday status... I hated those as well. Those things always remind me of what "could have" been, but I was forced to deal with what was: prison.

These continual wrestling matches of the soul proved to be more adversarial than the judicial system. At least with the system, it was doing what it was designed to do, but my soul was supposed to be my ally, but it was often my greatest tormentor. I hated that God allowed my imprisonment to persist, especially since He and I knew that I should have been dead at 16 instead of imprisoned with a life sentence. I guess His plan supersedes my own understanding.

I guess I had put a lot of credence on my co-defendant's lawyer, Eugene Pincham. He had told the court that, "if my client is forced to testify, this will only guarantee Mr. Gray a reversal." This made sense to me because he had an illustrious career as an appellate court judge prior to going into private practice. This was further, in my mind, plausible because my co-defendant's statement didn't inculpate (place guilt/blame) on me. The judge simply told him, "We'll let the Appellate Court deal with that." I figured I would shortly be receiving another reversal for this conviction, but I would be proven wrong.

I had once heard that hope was "dangerous", and I can attest to that being true somewhat, but I think that hopelessness is far more dangerous. I was preparing for yet another erroneous ruling; though I posited that it was less erroneous and more deliberate.

This is what the system did; it abused its powers over those who couldn't afford to effectively fight against it (and nowhere is this felt more than in my community). I felt pitiful because I kept seeing my hopes dashed by people who had been sworn to "uphold the constitution and law", but it seemed that the only thing that they really did was behave as if they were above it... I suppose they are.

It was sometime in January 2003 that Governor George Ryan issued a blanket Clemency to everyone on death row in Illinois. He would be imprisoned shortly thereafter and I always found it "coincidental" that they'd go after him after he'd exposed the arbitrariness of the death penalty sentence. He had been crooked long before they charged him, but it wasn't till after he called the system broken and granted Clemency did he then deserve to be incarcerated.

My latest cellmate, Caesar, was from "the row", yet I don't know what's worse, to be executed or to die slowly in prison in a cell no bigger than some people's closet. We'll all have varying opinions, but it's much better to die swiftly than slowly, or so I believe.

J.R. and I hadn't been cellmates for long due to the prison's "Secured Threat Gang" policy. They had him listed as folks and a c/o from around my hood had seen me one day during an interview after the tier I was on rioted, so he decided to tell the prison about my gang ties; thus I was re-designated as B.D. despite the fact that I had left them almost a decade ago. This meant only that when individuals align themselves with authority, fairness is often lost due to the guard's preconceived notions.

Missing You

It was very soon after that that I would be forced to deal with something no prisoner wants to deal with: death of a loved one. My step-dad had grown ill, and once he was taken to the hospital they diagnosed him with liver cancer. It was believed to be from over 30 years of drinking, despite one year of sobriety; I guess that wasn't enough to negate it. I kept standing in the gap between him and God; negotiating on some levels, but what did I really have that could be worth something? I even told God to take Eddie Sr. instead because I knew of the devastation that cancer causes a body; primarily because of what it did to my brother Steven when he was about 12 years old.

My mom came to see me one day; more somber than usual, but she told me, "Baby, Oscar died." I know people believe that if you expect death that it's easier to handle when it comes, but this isn't always the case. It seemed odd because initially they gave him about 2 years to live, but he didn't even make it to 6 months.

I kept a brave face for mom, this way I could console her, but the moment I was en route to the "cemented coffin" I resided in, I shed tears that I had long thought were dried up. It's an oddity that i always found ways to blame myself for the death of my loved ones, as if my incarceration were the cause of natural events or tragic events. Sitting in the cell, I pondered mom's words about him growing so sickly so quickly, he couldn't even understand that letter I had sent him. I wanted so badly to transfer my mom's pain onto myself, but I couldn't.

My mom was over 40 years old when she finally found a man who would love her the way she deserved, or at least the best he could. He had been taken by a disease so cruel and callous, that it almost seemed like another dimension of prison. He had been an integral part of my growth, despite what I morphed into. He once told me that, "Son... I hate like hell that yur in jail, but I'm grateful for it because you were killing your mother and me; being shot; being arrested; just being crazy. At least this place has allowed you to find yourself." I never forgot that; nor could I.

He meant FAR more to me than even my biological dad. It took for him to tell me that that even during my deprivation of opportunities, I could still find clarity.

I always pictured those two growing old together, especially since I was gone. I still hear his words here and there, like when he first visited me in the Juvenile Detention Center,: "Son, keep your head up because there ain't nothing on the ground worth looking at." Long before I met T.R. and even with me loving my grandma deeply, her living in Ohio took from that on some levels, but his presence was integral to growth on some levels. It's just that he came too late; the damage Eddie Sr. did was too enmeshed in my psyche.

I kept thinking about my "father's" death, but this kept me thinking about a work from Friedrich Nietchze -*Thus Spake Zarasuthrar** in which he said; "Few die too late, many die too early-die at the right time." I felt that he died too early, along with T.R., essentially everyone that I knew seemed to die "too early". That is, everyone but me. This was the hardest thing to understand because I had long wanted death, but it only evaded me to exacerbate my punishment of being alive. So now again I was being forced to lose a loved one; yet honestly, I felt that everyone would leave me, whether it was death or abandonment; they always leave.

---

*Friedrich Nietzche, Thus *Spoke Zarathustra, in The Portable Nietzsche*, trans. and ed. Walter Kaufman (New York: Penguin, 1976).

In my mourning I had been forced to deal with a new cell mate. Actually, Noah wasn't all that new because he had been my cellmate while I was in the county jail years prior to this. He was a young Mexican native who didn't speak English then (and I would miss those days of him not being able to talk). The comfortability (I use that word loosely.) of an individual's incarceration is largely based on their relationship with their cellmate. This is because you are literally in the cell with someone for roughly 20 hours of the day. Maybe he wouldn't have been so bad had I not been continually dealing with rejections from the court basically telling me I had no constitutional rights that they were bound to honor, like in the Dred Scott decision".

Though I didn't disbelieve God's plans for my life, it was hard to not allow my circumstance to test my faith. It seemed as if my faith was being choked by my pain; my pain was based on an unjust conviction, which in turn continued the feeling of inhaling radiation and chewing shards of glass. I tried to believe that even when I couldn't see God's hand, I could trust his heart though. The anguish didn't subside. Plus Noah complained over so many little things that it agitated me. It didn't matter that whatever I had he was welcomed to it, but he felt that "everybody owe me", but that's odd because a lot of the prisoners feel this way. I was the exact opposite of this because I felt the world didn't care enough about me to owe me anything.

But when we were talking, I'd try to console him from his fear of dying in prison (he had 80 years). But he had no desire to hear about a "loving God" who allowed him to be imprisoned; the oddity of this is he never claimed he was innocent. I tried to live as if I was godly but he once said," I don't respect guys who come to jail and find God." I told him he had that right, but had I been effectively exposed to God prior to jail I probably wouldn't have been locked up.

Chapter 8: Conscience

My serenity has almost always been inconsistent, but dealing with the constant negativity and accusations from him began to weigh me down to a point of me wanting to inflict physical harm on Noah. I hated the fact that who I once was is never really that far removed from who I am on any given day. So 1 had decided to take Tony up on his offer to get me a prison job. I told him that my initial declining of a job was before I had to spend hours with someone threatening my spiritual growth (in hindsight, he may have been helping me grow).

It took about a week before Tony was able to "pull some strings" and he had the unit where I was housed in Lieutenant give me an opportunity to work because Tony had worked for him when he was in Tony's unit. He initially told me that he didn't think that I would last because I went to several classes, but the job only entailed the duties of a janitor, so how could I not? He acted as if I would need to solve complex mathematical equations, or postulate theories of quantum physics. So I essentially achieved what I set out to do: get away from Noah. They moved the workers to the lower galleries, so I was moved within a week.

There were added advantages to working; we received an extra day of yard each week; we received a shower every day, and not only twice a week like the general population; though a "bird bath" can be effective, it wasn't a shower. But with these advantages, you had the disadvantages; like 200 guys in the unit presuming that you were their personal valet; antagonistic guards itching to show you that they are the "boss" over you. I hated dealing with so many personalities because inherently I'm introverted, but more importantly was my disdain of authority figures the reason for my displeasure of the job.

I hated that even my faith in Christ hadn't removed my disdain for almost anybody in a uniform; from a fireman, to a mailman or even a paramedic; if you wore one, I didn't like you. Though the police were hated the most. This sprang from not only what I heard they'd do to my brothers, you know, pulling them over just hassling them for being in "nice" cars, but what I endured by them even prior to my descent into criminality. My most vivid memory was when I was 13 years old and sitting on a friend's porch during the summer. It was about 7:00 p.m. so it was still light out; we were arguing over who was the best rapper from the group Niggas Wit' Attitudes (N.W.A) M.C. Ren or Ice Cube (Ren had my vote) when the police drove up and began asking questions, "What y'all doing? How come y'all ain't in the house?"

Before we even had a chance to respond to their questions, his mother was outside as if she smelled bacon permeating her house coming from outside. She began yelling, "This ain't South Africa; they on my porch, why y'all bothering them?' She had a few other unsavory words for them, but upon her requesting their badge numbers they sped off with such urgency that it seemed that they received a call saying the president had been shot and all units were needed. The moment she took their power from them by protecting rights we didn't know we had, they had to relinquish their antagonism. There were several instances of that nature (not all with a hero saving the day) that cemented my disdain for uniformed figures. I simply feel that the police are an extension of the courts; and I'm of no value to either, so this determines what they are to me. I was bound to reciprocate.

I had been working for a few months when my mom came up to visit me; the look of pain in her eyes and her not wanting to tell me something was wrong. The visiting room had one c/o in the back and one in the front; each table allowed for three visitors per prisoner, but there were only about 25 tables, so with a prison population of over 2,500, it was always crowded. I told her that I knew the pain in her eyes so well because I caused a lot of it, so it was a waste to try to hide it. After she told me, I almost wished that she didn't; my sister had been shot.

Sadly Sylvia wasn't aware of the obvious emotional instability of her latest boyfriend. My mom told me that she was on 100th and Emerald to visit some "friends" and that he apparently followed her and before she ever got a chance to depart the car, he fired up two shots at point-blank range. Though he left her for dead, she was enabled (I give God the credit) to make it to the door of her "friends" neighbor, who helped her inside and called the ambulance (I use quotations on friends because Sylvia said she believed they were home but didn't come to her aid). After being forced to digest this information I sat somberly; I was mostly upset that I couldn't exact vengeance on this guy as he deserved: nothing less than a slow and painful death.

My mother always tried to shield bad news from me, but I told her that I "needed to know stuff like this to help her share the emotional burden." She also said that she didn't want me to try to do anything to the guy if he'd come to Statesville; this is why she didn't give me his name after I asked for it. I did envision torture because I hadn't been this upset, not even over T.R.'s death. He died from a street element; drug spot and money, but this was something else. I hadn't wanted to torture someone since I chased a drug addict around with an axe because he owed me a couple hundred dollars; I only wanted to cut off his hands for his thievery.

It was clearly because of God's goodness that my sister survived because I couldn't imagine my niece Tanae as having lost both of her parents to murder. It seemed that the worst incidents have the best chance of causing for one to grow. I went through several live threatening situations pre and post incarceration. I initially figured it was the ineptitude of my enemies; but it was the grace of my God. This helped me because my current cellmate was a Christian brother who would play a role in my growth since Myke had recently been shipped to a medium security prison. And I needed the encouragement.

Richard had been incarcerated since I was 3 years old, so I empathized with him for being gone so long and I never would have imagined that I would be one of those. He used to tell me, "We can endure life's wrongs knowing that God will make them right." I believed that even though my circumstances caused for me to wrestle with guilt and innocence simultaneously, this ambivalence was enough to further confuse my fragile mental state. Though I would benefit from being in the cell with Richard, it wouldn't last, but I did gain from it.

And though all of my cellmates had played a role in my development, there would be one by whom my evolvement would surpass my own expectations because of. I often wondered how my evolvement as a man would have transpired had I not met him. T.K. was unlike the majority of prisoners; he had a Real Estate license; he had a Barber license; he was working on his Masters in Business Administration and he had taken courses on Criminal Justice; suffice it to say, books don't always keep you from prison. This elevated him in my eyes above the individuals I had been accustomed to dealing with. He and I got along quickly, whereas having a new cellmate can usually have anywhere between 2-3 week period of "feeling each other" out.

He used to ask me, "How can you reconcile Christianity with being so cynical?" He had a valid point, and I didn't mind listening because I knew that it wasn't malicious. I was forced to look at the anger I quietly (maybe not so quietly) held. This made me ponder what good were the several Bible Studies, Church Services and correspondence courses I had been taking. I never told him (or anyone) that my anger was based on my feelings, which were based on what I saw and that was based on what I saw each time I looked in the mirror: a 16 year old given life without parole. I had to make sure I didn't fall into the way a large majority of individuals in the prison demographic did: a stage of arrested development, meaning however old they were upon incarceration, this is the mentality they were stuck at. I promptly sought to not just chronologically age, but academically mature even more than I already had. T.K. wisely told me, "Your progress would only go as far as your social skills." This was an interesting thought.

I found that at this time I seemed to have undergone a virtual abandonment by my family (with the exception of mom). I'm glad that at this time a neighbor of Tony's; (also a grandmother of one of my (nephews) had begun writing me. Mrs. Jackson lived next to Tony, and I used to have animosity towards her because she'd call the police on us as we sold dope on the corner of her block (the nerve of her, right?). On a few instances prior to incarceration, she'd tell me, "Tony ain't gone do nothin' but get you in trouble." It's amazing how wise old people are because I would rue the day that he and I first talked. I was about 13 and me and one of his neighbors my age, Charles, snuck in his birthday party that he was throwing in his backyard. It was an 8 or 9 foot wooden fence enclosing the yard, so it was easy to sneak in. We'd peek through the cracks, and the moment the guys watching the entrance snuck away with some girl, we casually invited ourselves in. We only wanted to drink; and drink we did.

As I was working on my 3rd cup of beer from the keg, Tony walked up to me and said, "Ain't you one of them Gray's?" And the rest is history. It wouldn't be too long after that that I'd buy some dope from him to sell. I thought I wanted to be like him; he was living how I thought life should be lived; gold chains around his neck; taking different girls into his house seemingly every day; a mobile phone the size of a hybrid. I knew him because of my friend who lived on his block and his sister was in my class).

I was grateful for Mrs. Jackson at this time because it was easy to find a friend in prosperity, but seeing as I was in adversity, I needed one. I didn't minimize T.K.'s impact, but I enjoyed a spiritual component. T.K. and I had been cellmates for about a year when we went on a restriction because this July 11, 2007, hot and miserable day, a c/o had grabbed the shirt of one of the G.D.'s from 103rd. The guard was promptly beat to within an inch of his life, but once the other c/o's came, they returned the favor with the full justification of the prison; the fact that he was cuffed up didn't matter.

This gave me an opportunity to undertake a task that had long been whispering in my ear to do, even though I doubted my ability: writing a book. I had long been considered adept at writing poetry, or essays and raps, but this scared me. I also didn't trust the words of guys around here regarding my ability. A Dutch Philosopher Erasmus once said, "In the land of the blind, the one eyed man is king. "I simply took this to mean that if I was surrounded by unintelligent guys then what little smarts I may have had would only be highlighted: I still felt that it was time for me to go to work on something to better myself. Vincent Van Gogh said, "Great things are not done on impulse, but by a series of small things." I decided that I would at least try to do something good, if not great.

I was not expecting an opportunity to be working after our four month restriction was lifted. A c/o Lindsey, with whom I had grown cool while I was working, knew of the unfairness of my termination, and he decided to pull some strings to get it back for me. This is primarily because T.K. told me that I was an idiot for at first turning it down. He told me, "If you have someone who's willing to help you, let them." All the while my feelings of ineptitude were gnawing at my heels like a saboteur, but I pressed on. Because I had so many experiences in the streets, I felt it wouldn't be too hard to fictionalize it and after about 6 arduous months of creating characters; becoming familiar with the characters; trying to find satisfactory ways to end the characters, I would complete a work that my beloved Creative Writing teacher would enjoy. I felt like a dad in some way, whereas I had a vested interest in the ending of said characters; I was hurt when their ending didn't turn out how I wanted. But life doesn't always have room for "happy endings"; I can attest to that.

Even while I continued to work on legal endeavors, I began to draft another book. It was like my creativity was in overdrive, but I didn't want a book that would almost read like an urban novel, like the last one did (no disrespect to the genre), but I wanted to expose the subtle ways in which society propagated negative messages to my heritage. Subconsciously Unconscious would have to go into the ways in which legislation decimated our communities; it had to go into the false ideals propagated as the only way in which we should live and the half truths that schools in the country are satisfied with us receiving. This meant doing extensive research; giving statistics from the Department of Justice to validate what I have long suspected. I wanted to promote a positive message (despite being in a negative place). My intellect meant nothing if I didn't try to use it to help others.

I had began to wonder why didn't I take more time off before starting, but since prison by its definition seems to be an exercise in stagnancy, I felt writing would be a form of progress. As I kept pressing through the struggles of legal proceedings, the words of Frederick Douglas kept screaming in my head, "WITHOUT STRUGGLES, THERE IS NO PROGRESS." My research forced me to consider just how small I was in the grand scheme of injustice in America. I was often reminded that my spiritual positioning should not be overshadowed by my social concerns for my people, I just kept telling God that I could never attain "spiritual liberty while socially (imprisoned) bound"; nor did I want to be.

It was during this time that I continually considered myself as a blight to my family. I often felt that my murder would've simplified things for them; they could've shed tears and grieved, but that would be that. These feelings stemmed from a several month hiatus of even my mother visiting; all types of thoughts hit me, like if they love you, why aren't they doing all they can to try to help you to get out of prison?" This was worsened after I saw a PBS program that aired on May 9, 2007 titled "When Kids Get Life". It dealt with the juvenile life without parole question, but the oddity of the show was that it chronicled only Caucasians with this sentence, though they make up less than 5% of those given this. Studies have shown that youth of color are more likely to be arrested, detained, formally charged, and transferred to adult facilities and courts than their counterparts.

But in this documentary, the parents were extremely active in trying to get this legislation changed; it seemed that African - Americans go under some defeated ideology that "if the courts do it, it must be right." Sadly, this ideology extends to more than court dealings. I had figured that since I was incarcerated so young; this prevented them from having any long term obligations to be loyal. I may have been simply looking for an excuse for their behavior. I wondered wasn't I the same little 8-9 year old that my brothers swung in a circle till I was dizzy to mimic "Superman"; wasn't I the same little brother that would grab my brother's arm only to receive an exaggerated movement as we wrestled, with them screaming "UNCLE" giving me a victory I had no idea I didn't deserve; wasn't I the same little brother that my sister would trick into her room, and then she and her friends would tickle me and kiss me knowing that I thought girls were "gross"? I guess I wasn't.

I guess I alone can receive the blame for that because no force was used to make me an alcoholic, drug dealing lunatic. The depression was so palpable that it caused me to stop writing *Subconsciously Unconscious* almost as quickly as I started writing it. I had felt that it was a waste of time, because I wanted to go "harder" on my legal proceedings. I had been given access to seemingly esoteric legal information because T.K. had worked in the prison law library and he had been allowed to bring the books back for the weekend. I took advantage of such a privilege. I sought my freedom with as much tenacity as I sought my enemies because something far more important than my anger was at stake: my right to live outside of prison.

I didn't really like pondering the fact that I couldn't beat the unjust conviction alone, but I noticed that it was never far removed from my mind. They had been wrongfully imprisoning guys for longer than I had lived, so it was daunting to consider this especially in knowing the court appointed lawyers had little interest in a guy's innocence; maybe they didn't have the time to care. The consistent false imprisonments were constantly shown and any objective observation could verify it; the saying, "Just because you're paranoid doesn't mean no one is watching you" comes to mind.

I had also been continually writing to various Innocence Projects in an effort to obtain help; the consensus was that since I had two separate murder convictions they were unwilling to help me on either (I have no rationale behind that). Fortunately, the books T.K. had been sharing with me helped me to expand my legal acumen, but unfortunately because I was pro se (representing self) it meant nothing. This simply meant that I was swinging at the air with the expectation of knocking it down; I suppose that would've been easier than fighting the courts.

Before T.K. and I were going to our respective assignments this September 3, 2008 morning; we were told that we would be moved to different cells. I was agitated because he seemed to have been the only family I had left; Myke did consistently have his sister send me $100.00 every other month. And Tony had recently been sent to Menard prison because one of his close associates at the prison with him was "allegedly" having a female bring them contraband items in, and since they couldn't catch any of this imagined contraband, they simply shipped everybody that hung around them. I knew that T.K. and I were being moved because the unit's staff didn't like walking up the stairs to get us out for our jobs; I had recently been assigned to the commissary.

The fact that I had been taken away from the (closest) family I had was going to complicate my legal proceedings because he had been integral in my legal evolvement. My current post conviction petition had been pending over seven years; I always equated these long periods as being beneficial to me; clearly I was always wrong. I had continually sought the elusive "justice" because at this point I had spent literally 50% of my existence incarcerated. I wanted this to be corrected as soon as possible without suicide. I had discovered that fighting the system was like swimming in quicksand and then by some miracle making it to shore, I find that it's inhabited by deaf and blind occupants; much like the fabled "Lady Justice" was because she's not only blind, but she's deaf to the truth of my innocence.

I had the tendency to allow for my negative rulings to dictate my spiritual meter, but it just seemed that the pain from them made me feel as if I were being amputated at the knees without anesthesia, then salt was poured into the wounds; and then the courts telling me that I can't scream and it was against the law to try to crawl. Though I only allowed for this to be the case briefly; I mean the disappointment and depression would subside, my agitation increased daily because no amount of God consciousness would negate that fact. True, my spirit was convinced in God's ability, but my natural circumstances are what I allowed to take center stage to perform an encore performance of, *Psychological Torture: A Broadway Play*, starring Marcos Gray and directed by life.

I know this may seem contradictory to a faithful believer in Christ, but the fact remains that my sanity was hanging by a thread thinner than a balding man's hair. It was during this time that I would be moved to segregation to work. This building made the other units seem sanitary in comparison (this says a lot) because it had more roaches than China had people; it had mice the size of babies; it was the only panopticon in the state. (The panopticon was first established in 1826 in Western State Penitentiary; it was a huge circular tower that the guard would be in to give the impression that he was capable of watching the inmates that were housed on all four sides of the building; thus inmates would literally "police" themselves out of fear that the guard was watching).

My first reaction to going to work in "seg" was who I was going to have to beat into a coma if someone "shot" me with one of their "guns". These guns were made from plastic bottles, rubber bands and a few other non-descript items. I would have preferred the bullets regular guns shot, but these guns shot feces at whomever the "triggerman" didn't like. I found that thought funny in a way because it exposed just how far from being like Christ I actually was. The past violent predilections may not be on my surface, but there was a possibility of them showing up at any moment...to my dismay.

This preconceived idea of seg exposed to me that I was doing the same thing that society had done to me by the juries that kept convicting me; in their defense, there was a modicum of truth to my depravity, there just was no proof to these specific acts as being mine. My 6 month rotation over there went mostly without incident, except for an individual murdering their cellmate because he believed that he was stealing from him. There is a prison creed that states, "stealing carries no probation"; this means that it should be penalized most severely. The thing that compounded this 24 year olds death was that he had only 46 days left until he went home. The uncertainty of this place is often lost in its monotony because each day could literally be your last.

Man In The Mirror.

I'm certain that I wasn't the only one to have been shocked by the sudden demise of Michael Jackson on June 25, 2009. I have to admit, that prior to his death I couldn't tell you when was the last time I thought about him; even if after listening to my *Thriller* or *Off The Wall* tapes (yes, we still use those). I found it odd because his death resonated more deeply with me than 2Pac's did, and next to the Bible, 2Pac's words were the "gospel truth". When 2Pac died in 1996, I simply pulled a couch to the wall while I was in the county jail and remembered (as much as I could) what I was doing while listening to his songs, but the death of Mike seemed to cause for me to extrapolate memories of me 7 or 8 years old being dressed in church clothes or a Thriller jacket dancing to try to entertain some of my siblings. It seemed that with his demise I was forced to realize the actuality of my entire innocence was gone with it; I guess a double murder conviction wasn't enough.

As I mourned Mike more than he probably deserved, I felt that my energy would be better spent on trying to do something (anything) on trying to manifest my freedom. Ironically I would receive a call from a Public Defender (P.D.) telling me that my brief that had been pending almost 10 years was frivolous; had this been true the courts would've thrown it out years ago since the prosecution filed a motion to dismiss and the (then) judge denied it. The legal strength of my issues was well documented in Illinois and his attempts at sabotage were clear. I had known that just because a P.D. was appointed, this didn't mean that they had your best interest in mind. I've had a fair share of lawyers who cared nothing for my innocence; in fact, they seemed to willingly operate as the prosecutor. Or maybe they were just overwhelmed at the sheer number of people they're forced to represent.

I was beginning to fear the fact that maybe I hated prison more than I loved God. But this feeling has been the motivation to try to obtain my exoneration because I didn't like every time I looked in the mirror I saw the face of the 16 year old reflected telling me that I should NEVER touch foot in society. Nor did the 16 year old reflected mean that I could pass for 16; the Gray hairs on my beard since my 20's would see to that. This was what I fought against; a head full of gray hair upon release. This sentence and its permission of youth dying slowly in prison is worst (to me) than the concentration camps because that was a sure death instead of a long drawn out one; God forbid a juvenile serving life live to be 100 years old.

I noticed that often times the laws that should be the catalyst for my relief was simply ignored by the courts because I was the one to have brought it to their attention. My being ignored tortured me daily, but this was why I was always under some type of compulsion to try to extricate myself from a prison cell, rather a "cemented coffin" is more accurate. I've always seemed to have had difficulties with waiting on God, so I was in a constant game of "hide-go-seek" with justice, but it was like I was looking for her in Illinois and she wasn't even in the country. The P.D. told me that the state's attorney would file their Motion to Dismiss and it would probably be granted. Despite the case law supporting my position, since it was my position, it was granted. A pro se filing may as well say, "Blah, blah, blah" because that was how the courts treated it.

I even had the P.D. tell the judge that I wanted to go pro se in order to not have valid issues waived; she wasn't hearing any of that. I kept hearing T.K.'s voice telling me, "You need to go pro se" but my feelings of ineptitude touched every facet of my existence. I rationalized that it may not have made a difference, but I owed it to my life to try. I kept being hit with the reality that the more I claimed to have placed it in God's hands, the more I snatched my case back from Him. The Bible verse in Revelation 3 v.7 kept coming to mind, "He opens the door that no man can close, He closes the door that no man can open." Yet, my knowledge of this fact didn't stop me from trying to part these walls like Moses had done the Red Sea (though it was God using Moses to part it).

I felt that God could understand that life in prison as a kid added a degree of desperation; clearly His mercy could understand my position. This last negative ruling made me feel as if I were constantly screaming at the top of my lungs, but the courts didn't respond because they told me all that they heard was an echo lingering in the ethers. I didn't care because the extent of my existence would NOT be what they wanted it to be; though it was the bane of my existence it would not be its culmination.

T.K. and I had been moved back into the cell with one another, and I knew that I would take his advice to go pro se the next time; with me there was always going to be a next time. I knew it was a risk, but it was no riskier than what I've been enduring because judges tend to make erroneous (intentional) rulings with impunity, so why should they stop? I was reluctant to accept an assignment in the gym because I thought that it would impede my multiple endeavors, but it wouldn't. Though on 5 nights a week we'd have to stay till 5:30p.m. to clean up the gym and on weekends we'd have to set up the electrical equipment for the services that ran on weekends. This took a total of an hour for us four workers. I'd go up to the upper room to do my legal research or assignment from various correspondence courses. The room had an air conditioner, a desk with a chair, 12 chairs for the students of the classes taught and a motivating aura for me.

There were several other benefits as well; I'd been allowed access to free weights that the general population wasn't; I was allowed to see everyone from other units because they all had gym on different days, but the solitude in doing my legal work was the most priceless. It. wasn't too long after I started working in the gym that I would be awakened this August 13, 2010 to be told that I was going to court, or as it's called a 'writ'. I didn't know that the motion I had filed requesting to go pro se would mean that the judge would need for me to state this on the record for confirmation. This gave me another chance to hope for the manifestations to the prayers I'd been sending up to the ceiling hoping that God would enter the cell I resided in so that He could hear them.

The preparation by the guards entailed handcuffing me, with the right palm facing upward and the left down; a steel box around the cuffs to further restrict movement; a heavy chain around my waist that would be attached to the cuffs and a 5 pound bell around my waist to compliment the leg shackles. The obvious aspect is that the cuffs and the shackles cut into your skin with the slightest movement and the fact that the guards have you by the chain makes it feel like it's a leash; in reality, that's exactly what it is. I always feel like Hannibal Lecter going on writs, but sadly, I've not had the opportunity to meet Jodie Foster.

While driving in physical pain, I would soon be confronted by mental pains; seeing people driving places; seeing half dressed women walking places; seeing people essentially enjoying the mundane aspects of life while I was on my way to try to fight for that privilege. Though the ride was about 90 minutes, it seemed even longer because of what my mind was wrestling with based upon, not just what I saw going to court, but with the individuals with whom I was being transported to court, parole violators crying about the few months or 2 years of parole time they were facing while I sat wallowing in the reality that we didn't just die in the streets, but we were dying in prison as well; we were dying more slowly however.

As I made it into the court room, I was surprised that my usual nervousness was gone. I don't know if my faith in God had grown; or if my faith in myself had grown or had my psychosis resurfaced. I came to learn that my judge had recently been promoted from a prosecutor (as most judges), so this didn't bother me as much as it could've. She had asked me, "Mr. Gray, why do you want to represent yourself? Do you have a law degree?" I know in hindsight I may have erred, but instinctively I said, "No, but my P.D. doesn't act like he has one so I'm in no worst position." I had long known that sarcasm wasn't appreciated by everyone, but it was how I felt. She simply smirked and gave me a three month continuance to begin the "Merry-Go-Round" of appellate procedures; I wished that I could simply jump off.

After my initial convictions I no longer held on to the illusions about truth and justice in the criminal courts; innocence often seemed to be of little importance. The only thing that was dispersed from the courts direction seemed to be systematic injustice. I owed it to my faith to believe God's words; He said "NO weapon formed against me shall prosper; every false tongue shall be condemned" (Isaiah 54 v 17) and I believed it. I noticed that my embarking on this journey in the courts was like my foot was stuck in wet cement, but the more I tried to get away the deeper I would be sucked in; the quicker I was expediting my demise. A voice told me that, "As long as you struggle against imprisonment, the longer it'll last"; I quickly chalked that up to Satan.

As I went through the motions of these proceedings, a shocker occurred that not only impacted the prison population, but the entire prison as well. My beloved Creative Writing teacher, Dr. Margaret T. Burroughs, passed away in December 2010 at the age of 92. She had been teaching at the prison since 1989. She had, along with her husband, created the Ebony Museum of Negro History in 1961 (later changed to DuSable Museum of African American History named after Jean Baptiste DuSable, the founder of Chicago). She had a day named after her by the late Chicago Mayor Harold Washington on February 1, 1986; she'd received many awards and honors for her achievements, such as a Doctorate of Human Letters from Lewis University, Honorary degree from the Arts Institute of Chicago and her Bachelors and Masters of Fine Art from several other colleges. But it was her love for her pupils at the prison that shined the most brightly when discussing. We all affectionately called her "mother" because of her unwavering love for us, which society had relegated us to its "throwaways"; its derelicts, but not to her. Though she was only about five feet tall and 110 pounds with 10 pounds of weights on her; her hugs still seemed to engulf us; it is this person who helped me believe that I could say things of relevance.

Chapter 9: Battle Scars

This latest death forced me to ponder on the mortality of my own mother; the realization dawned on me that I wasn't the only one aging by the decades, but my mother was as well. I don't imply that this caused for me to go into "overdrive" with regards to trying to find my release from prison, but it did cause for me to be more anxious with what I already had pending in court. The truth on my side was constantly dismissed simply because I was the one speaking it, rather revealing it in my legal petitions. My humanity was easily disregarded because of my geographical location: prison. But the saddest part of the stereotypes about prisoners is that often they exemplify all of the negative traits society believes about them anyway.

Though I was grateful that I was no longer what I was at one point, I was aware that my human frailties that followed me from adolescence were never far away; this is why I felt that I needed to have a hand in securing my release. It always was present in the back of my mind that without God's help, my circumstance would probably remain as it was hopeless and imprisoned. The oddity about worrying about my mother's death at this time was that it would be my biological dad's death that would creep up on me. He passed away December 22, 2010 (or as I call that day, the 16th anniversary of T.R.'s murder). He had been battling cancer for years and as with many cancer patients, they often lose. This caused me to recall October 10, 1997, I was on the phone with my sister and he was there visiting and we began to talk. I didn't tell him that I felt that everything in my life that went wrong was because of him (though I believed this). The date is indelibly etched in my memory because this was the only time I EVER heard him tell me that he loved me; clearly this meant that I didn't believe it.

Fortunately, Christ had been working on my heart so I told him that I loved him as well; I meant it. Though it was (is) with a hint of ambivalence because I loved him because God expected me to, but I hated him for my very conception because I felt that I would have served the world much better had I been secreted on a sheet. It was odd because only a few years prior to him telling me that he loved me I couldn't have cared less, but I did have some love for him despite his harsh treatment towards my mother and my siblings, but ESPECIALLY me. I hated that my imprisonment didn't allow me to try to show such a Christ-like demeanor that I would guilt him into apologizing, but since I had been incarcerated over 17 years at the time of his death and he'd never attempted to visit me, I suppose that I had long been dead to him. He was now reciprocating. And oddly, I wasn't as glad as I thought I was going to be.

The prison showed the movie *Conviction* on April 28, 2011 and I found it ironic because that was the date in which I was first convicted for a murder I didn't commit. The movie starred Hillary Swank as a woman whose brother had been locked up for a murder she didn't believe he committed. She believed so strongly in his innocence that she went to school to get her G.E.D.; she went to school to get her college degree; she then went on to law school to get a degree in order to prove his innocence. Obviously, this wasn't an easy task, and it strained her relationship with her husband and kids, but this was something she felt she "needed" to do to get her brother out of jail and she finally succeeded and after 18 years of prison existence, he was allowed to walk free.

I shed a few tears after the movie (I expose this at the risk of seeming "soft"), but not for the 18 years that he spent in jail (I was in my 18th year), but for the fact that it caused me to consider how little support I received from my siblings. I guess since I was so stubborn prior to imprisonment, they feel as if I had failed them on some levels (I did). I felt that maybe this negated any loyalty they may have owed me, but I had long known that blood relations didn't make one loyal. And since that didn't translate into loyalty, I couldn't expect for it to transfer anything less than their behavior from their children; the next generation of my family that I affected by my imprisonment. But just because I understood this didn't mean it didn't hurt all the same. I knew how unreasonable it was to expect for that movie to be replicated; but a semblance of support would have been welcomed, and not just the occasional birthday card or money. I guess they were saying, without opening their mouths, was that my death in prison was acceptable. I was forced to face the reality that I had to depend on God

TOTALLY for my vindication. The anger, hurt, and pain and desperation sat down in my mind like an unwanted houseguest who didn't know when to leave; this was the crux of my prison existence. I felt like French novelist Alexander Dumas Pere's character in *The Count of Monte Cristo*, where he said, "Woe to those who put me in this wretched prison and woe to the people who forgot I was there." You understand how damaging this was to my spirit; it sabotaged my growth exposing my frailties again. My spiritual position and my physical position were at war, but I had to be mindful that I didn't want my spirit man to be the casualty; even though he was on life support.

While continuing to contend with my spiritual growth; my legal problems; with my indifferent family, I focused on publishing a book I'd written; *Subconsciously Unconscious* was substantiated with statistics validating the deplorable conditions my community faced and its impact on past and present generations. The publishers I had told me (without always saying it) that they weren't interested as I was saying it; it's ignored simply because I (a prisoner) was saying it; it felt like they took a page from the judges in my legal proceedings. This was unfortunate, but it caused me to simply self publish because if I didn't invest in myself then I couldn't really expect for someone else to. I was fortunate to have had the funds because of Myke having his sister send me some of his money every few months, plus the prison job(s) I had been working.

I felt that if I didn't try to use what little knowledge I had in order to help someone else then I really had no purpose in existing; this doesn't imply I actually felt I had a purpose, but it could help me forget how empty my existence was. I also suppose that on some levels I was so adamant in trying to succeed in publishing to offset my constant failures at the litigation stage in court. I wanted to make someone's existence better by having been here, but I felt that the only way to accomplish this was by teaching them that it was never too late to evolve as a person. But no sooner than I found an affordable self publishing company, I was being forced to set that aside and deal with a prosecutor's Motion to Dismiss my current post conviction petition, which had been filed over 9 years prior. Even though this motion was technically collateral estoppel (filed before and ruled in my favor) the judge would allow it in CLEAR violation of the law.

The procedures I went through when responding to a prosecutor's motions were to see if the cases they cited were valid, or had they been merely taking words and phrases out of context (they often did). I would then locate cases to support my position and see if they applied to my case. If the concept of "justice" was as practical in our society as it was theoretical, I wouldn't have had any doubts as to the outcome, but my experiences with the system showed me otherwise so I stayed suspicious of the judge(s). But I acted simply due to the fact that without action, there isn't even a chance of success. I had felt that I had to act in order to remove the onus of a bogus conviction from my life.

I was glad that I felt a purpose for my actions because I simply felt that prison was an exercise in non-existence; I'm like a ghost; I'm here, but I'm not. Warfare, for all intents and purposes, has a set of rules upon which the parties abide by (i.e. Geneva Convention), but when battling the courts, it's hard ESPECIALLY pro se. But I guess if the only other alternative is to die in prison, this simplifies the route one must take. In "honest" warfare, we have an aggressor, but you knew the enemy, but in judicial warfare - it's different because the person who is supposed to be neutral (judges) often take up the role of the prosecutor. I suppose that since most of them were prosecutors make it hard to change their thoughts about prisoners.

The judicial system has a well documented history of misapplying the law for the prosecutor's benefit, and simultaneously disregarding it when it benefits the incarcerated. The practice of arbitrariness and hypocrisy is seen so frequently that it surprises no objective observer; maybe this indicts our society as being unobjective. They seem content with believing in the mythical "justice" with as much eagerness as children believing in Santa Claus; without any thought on the improbability of an obese man sliding down a chimney to leave gifts and then flying away on magical reindeers. I guess if society can believe in "justice", children should be taught of Santa Claus in history class as an actual person, and not a person based on a person.

My court day came on November 21, 2011 without any fanfare; merely 8 days after my birthday. The ever present feeling I had was that my day of birth should never be celebrated, but instead they should have lit candles in vigils to grieve it. The customary disregard from the courts was always present; I had no lawyer advising me on what would be the best strategy I should take; no false presumption that the judge was going to rule correctly; and I had a sickening feeling that the court room was going to play out like a scene from the movie *Gladiator*, with me playing Russell Crowe's character Maximus, yet I had no physical weapons to force my enemy to its knees (in the form of ruling correctly). And my judge was my main antagonist, portrayed by Joaquin Phoenix (Marcus Aurelius).

Sadly, I felt just like Maximus when Aurelius poisoned him outside of the spectators view, but then released him from his chains to fight him in view of the audience to give the illusory aspect of a fair fight. But I had no spectators screaming for my release because I fought valiantly; there were merely indifferent people deeming me only an unpitiable sacrifice placed (again) on a judicial systems altar. It seemed as it often did that my research and case law that supported my position was of no consequence; it seemed as if I was always at the "mercy" of a biased judge's opinion, and not by the law they swore to uphold. And if a court isn't bound by rules, it isn't bound by facts and the court proceedings are no longer based on dispensing "justice", but it's merely an issue of men and our fates depend not on guilt or innocence, but on whom you know or don't know, or what mood a judge is in.

Though the judge's antagonistic treatment, towards me was visible from the outset, I still allowed for my faith to be strengthened by hope, despite reality. I felt foolish for believing that the judge would uphold the rule of law; instead she bound my hands for the prosecutor to place my neck in a noose in order for me to be (yet again) a victim of a judicial lynching. I must admit that she was consistent in her animus towards me, but I didn't allow that to totally destroy my faith in God's deliverance. I felt (feel) that at some point I have to attain the exoneration that hides. I wasn't as mad at God as I thought I would be, I did ponder just how much did he care for me with him allowing this to constantly replicate itself in my legal proceedings.

It was nothing else for me to do but acclimate my mind for yet another round, but I believed as Nazi General Von Stuelpanasel; "No defeat is final, but simply a lesson to be learned." Far be it from me to quote a

Nazi General, but I agreed with that assessment, but for the life of me, I just couldn't figure out what God was still trying to show me; was He trying to show me how-to fail? If so, He was wasting His time because I felt that my entire being was a failure.

Though I probably will never be able to understand things as I would like to, I had to keep focused. While I was being driven back to the cemented coffin that warehoused me, the scenery seemed much bleaker; the beautiful women I was seeing had all seemed to turn into Medusa, thus forbidding me from looking them directly into the eyes. But honestly, it was shame that caused that. And as used to negative rulings as I had been accustomed to, I still was never going to be used to them because I believed in my innocence, but this was hard being in the mouth of a system that seemed like a dragon that feigns hunger, but actually it was only gluttonous, devouring every piece of flesh it can, but it had a penchant for dark meat. I had no choice, however, but to fight to be regurgitated from this beast; I had to fight against the kidnapping (literally) that took place when I was 16 years old; sadly, all of my efforts at "kicking and screaming" through the legal proceedings seemed to fall on deaf ears.

But as I kick and scream, I only receive indifferent looks from the courts (and society) telling me simply to accept my plight because the only "ransom" to satisfy my captors is my death in prison; there will be no release if they have it their way. But as I looked at the clouds that seemed to turn red as soon as I stepped foot outside, I knew the battle was still waging; and it would be so as long as I breathed inside of a prison cell. I would devote my last breath to getting out; even if I had to do it by myself .Because as it stands, a prison existence is comparable to residing inside of a cemetery where its "zombies" seek "re-animation" through judicial procedures; yet, all the while knowing that this very judicial process seeks our "death" by depriving us of the justice they claim we have.

Conclusion: Written In Blood

I initially wondered how do I interest a demographic that does not believe in my story as having any consequence to their lives. But whether they want to face it or not, I am a "face of the nation." I am conscious that they would rather not acknowledge my face for fear that it would eat at their conscience. I knew that in order for my story to be told, then it would have to be by me that my story was told. My story left to the hands of anyone else would simply be told as one of infamy. Society needs to know that they too are affected by my story. I'm under the belief that they are often ignorant as to the harsh sentencing schemes employed on juveniles in this country alone. But even with this sentence, I fight to retain my humanity. The humanity I've attained since being imprisoned is usually negated by my very imprisonment (in society's eyes) because society is allowed to go under a premise that my humanity is less than theirs; or that my pain is less than theirs; and that my imprisonment automatically implies I deserve whatever I received from the courts (juvenile or not).

Imprisonment has the capacity to destroy hope, but compound that with an unjust imprisonment and you'll see rocket fuel being sprinkled on sticks of dynamite: pure destruction. My anguish has been compounded by the duration of my imprisonment; nevertheless I've had to allow for the imprisonment to help me be a better version of whatever it is that I once was. I've had to be mindful of what I've become and how I've become it. My progression is not a one-time event because I've yet to reach the final stage of my metamorphosis to become who I'm destined to be. Though on many levels, my past is a nightmare from which I can't escape, it weighs me down like an anchor attached to my ankle tossing me overboard from the "ship", better known as society. My past seems to whisper in my ears, "You will NEVER be anything." This is the juvenile life sentence, which essentially took away my chance to be a productive member of society; a husband; a father; it took away my chance to simply...be.

In contending with that, I also fight with my representation, of God and that I can't be who and what I once was by not thinking about consequences. After all, non-thinking is a form of genocide. Prior to prison, I was full of anger, pain, and hatred (not to imply I've totally defeated those) and I allowed it to morph into violence to conceal the anguish of my existence. I had to realize that my future wasn't dependent on anything I do, but on what God does. It's never far from my conscious that my convictions are not based on what I actually did, but nor is it far from my conscious that someone is probably incarcerated for things I actually did. Still, these types of sentences don't offer any cures to the continuity of juvenile criminality. If we fail to attack the "why?" a crime is committed by juveniles, prison will never be a deterrent.

It is not my intention to glorify my past behavior, but to express how even in an abysmal place such as prison, there is redemption. I found it odd because I thought I was beyond redemption; this life sentence posits I'm beyond redemption, "but with God, all things are possible" (Matthew 19 v 26). This belief alone makes the fight with the courts worthwhile. At the same time, I try to embody the late, great Maya Angelou's words, "I believe that your legacy is every life you are able to touch while you were privileged to be here on this earth." I have to "touch" people's lives positively, even though my emotional state is comparable to a pendulum swinging back and forth between my faith in God's deliverance and abject depression feeding me the thought that it should culminate in suicide.

I can't allow for the anguish to detract from the purpose God has for me. I believe there is some sanctity in my suffering, because it seems as if whatever "good" I may have had at one point in my life prior to incarceration had to dissipate in order for something greater to take its place. Although it would take prison for that evolution of character. As if the entire substance of my life HAD to be tragic, and not just the beginning. At 16 years old, some could posit that my life was merely on the cusp of beginning; my birth implied potential, but it was negated by environmental factors, that culminated in my being in prison wrestling with what I had become: a juvenile lifer. The conflict persists because it is so easy to say what I should have done differently, or not done at all, but growing up as I did, I gauged consequences by whether it ended in death or not. Nothing else mattered because prior to prison, I was always on the precipice of death; strangely, prison pulled me from its perch.

But with that being said, we still must question the JLWOP (and its equivalents) because they don't coincide to what we know about juveniles. The psychological differences between juveniles and adults has long been known, but the United States Supreme Court in <u>Miller v Alabama</u>, 567 U.S. at ___, ___ 132 S.Ct. 2464 and <u>Graham v Florida</u>, 560 U.S. 98,59 (2010) simply brought it further into legal context. Yet even before those rulings, society had placed prohibitions on kids voting, joining the army, marrying, drinking, and a plethora of other privileges based upon their inherent immaturity, but to posit these same kids could spend the rest of their lives in prison is an exercise in hypocrisy. How can people cling to the notion that the aforementioned freedoms be enjoyed by people only 18 years old and older, but not to children who are allowed to serve life sentences or sentences that mount up to life?

So not only is the application of those sentences abhorrent, but so is the arbitrary and prejudicial manner in which it is implemented. According to *#15 to Life: Kenneths Story* at PBS.Play.org, "Blacks are ten times more likely to receive life than their white counter parts." I strongly believe that if a nation's judicial system is indicative of its moral fiber, then our nation's moral fiber is weakened by such sentences. How can we espouse "equality" or "fairness" by this disproportionate application; not to mention its application in general? Political Theorist Tommie Shelby stated, "Individuals are forced to make choices in an environment they did not choose. They would surely prefer to have a broader array of good opportunities. The question we should be asking, not instead of, but in addition to questions about penal policy is whether the denizens of the ghetto are entitled to a better set of options, and if so, whose responsibility is it to provide them?"[2]

How can one measure the effects of an individual's environment? I may not be academically adept at doing so, but from an experiential standpoint, I know that there is a correlation between environment and crime. I don't subscribe to the notion that no penalty should be issued juvenile offenders, but the U.S. Constitution states there should be "no cruel and unusual punishment" (8th Amendment) and the Illinois

Constitution states penalties must be implemented to "consider the youthfulness of the offender and restore them to useful citizenship"(Article 1 Section 11). These sentences can't do that. And are inherently "cruel and unusual."

Since the federal and state constitutions are ignored, and the sentences don't deter juvenile criminality, we must look at the situation holistically. I concur with the poignant words of Michelle Alexander, "We can choose to be a nation that extends care, compassion, and concern to those who are locked up and locked out and headed to prison before they are old enough to vote."[3] I strongly believe that the general consensus from society is that it's acceptable because it disproportionately impacts only African-American communities; depleting communities of their children and children of their potential. All of this is accepted if it posits "tough on crime". Martin Luther King Jr. stated, "One of the greatest tragedies of man's long trek along the highway of history has been limiting of neighborly concern to tribe, race, class or nation. The consequences of this narrow, insular attitude are that one does not really mind what happens to people outside of his group.[4]

Will we be able to prove Dr. King wrong, because as it stands, the reality of society's indifference makes me feel as if I would have fared better in a country that didn't espouse "freedom, justice for all", while simultaneously practicing hypocrisy and cruelty under the guise of legislation. It sickens me, further creating an embittered soul towards it because I know that I'm one of the lowest members of an unspoken caste system; I'm the lowest on society's "totem pole" because of my heritage. I'm an African-American male, thus I'm the wretched of the earth. Or maybe this is what my story tells me about my life because of my prison sentence. This creates a story which has been essentially written in blood, a story that is read in regret because that which is placed before me is a chasm separating me from society so vast that there seems to be no way for me to cross it. Yet, even with all of that, I still fell the onus is on me to combat the tears that fertilize the soil of my heart and the growing self-hatred and pain due to my incarceration. Until I do this (combat and be victorious for my peace) maybe my story will remain as it is. I do believe that my faith in God will not be so easily defeated, nor will my quest for redemption.

Bibliography

1. <u>Scot v Sanford</u>, (Dred Scot Decision) 60 U.S. 393, 15 L.ed 691 (1857) "A black man has no rights that a white man is bound to respect."

2. Carl E. Pope and William Feyerherm- <u>Minority Status and Juvenile Justice Processing</u>: An Assessment of the Research Literature.

3. Michelle Alexander- <u>The New Jim Crow: Mass Incarceration in the Age of Color-blindedness</u>, New Press, pg. 206

4. Martin Luther King Jr.-<u>Strength to Love</u>, Philadelphia Fortress Press, pgs. 31-2

Lost Innocence: The Life of a Juvenile Lifer

Juvenile Life Without Parole

I internalize the anguish, which is why I'm still scarred,

They may trickle down to my writings, which is why to read them, sometimes it's so hard.

They designed like an airbag-for impact,

effectively at dressing things society wishes for you to disregard; clearly a conscience they lack.

Juvenile with life and no parole,

legislatively designating me to a life with no goals, like a body with no soul,

pretty much simply like finding the dead sea, without finding the dead sea scrolls,

like they don't care for its effects on me or my community, like my disappearance has no toll.

Surprisingly, God has raised for me to rise and be, compassionate; no longer cold.

To the death I fight to be free; I won't fold,

so it's nothing, else for me to be, but like Christ; made in a new mold.

In his image, subtract the definition of a menace, as the D.A. propagated,

They wanted my life nullified, before I was to begin it, of course

I hate it, this life? If I had to grade it?

an F plus plus,

why didn't they just bring the noose into the court room

and eliminate the theatrics, and let death rush, rush ,

life from my body, a quick asphyxiation, the psychological devastation,

caused because I endure life without parole in this hypocritical

nation-as a juvenile.

Marcos 2-11-13

The Killing Fields

There could be no transference to the the disturbance...upon which My existence yields...

I concocted ways to assuage my guilt for the cataclysm that I Constructed... for the destruction that I was prone to build.

I was raised in a war zone...a veritable killing field...we were Like the Cambodian Khmer Rouge...

Always prepared to use violence as conflict resolution... so depravity and dejection...manifested itself...in a deluge.

These confrontations yielded complications... for the rest of my Days. .
.

Though I sought my physical extermination I was met with a social Eradication due to my designation...inside of a prison's cage...

Yet the implications... were subtle...the trouble was in my ideology... I lived violently with no apology for having acclimated my psychology To the street's philosophy... prognosis psychopathy.

So how do I create life in the streets that I created destruction In...

I suppose that in the resurrection of goals that I didn't think I deserved to have... I manufactured corruption... but it was victorious Because against it... I could not win.

So with every line that I send up to God... I pray that my sins will be forgiven...

It's very hard to have guilt over blood that I never spilt... but I do nave genuine remorse over the fact... that I am still living. Rather, existing inside of this dilapidated cemented coffin for Me did they build...

And for those who look like me under a false premise that this...

Would offset Chicago's killing fields... but it didn't... not for real

.

I Know Why The Caged Brothers Scream pt 2

Sadly I brood... never in the mood for happiness since the shrapnel Of pain disperses throughout my every pore...

This causes for me to give up the thing that I couldn't afford...

My very life... so now my entire existence is living out... the Art of War. I question, my evolvement as a man... and can. I accomplish any great Feats... or will my adolescent mistakes deplete...

Me of any hope... and if it does so, does this mean that I am weak?

How can I exist when my life subsists of nothing... but debilitating Pain...

And my wings of hope have not merely been broke...

but doused with gasoline... and they expect me to smile as I endure

These flames.

Though I was raised to be enraged... this isn't simply for any exegetical purpose.. .despite what I term the inevitable... my self Destruction... because in my reflection... I see only my worthlessness.

But God said that my curse is intertwined with my blessing, yet Kleptomaniacal was my upbringing...

Which has left me inside of a "cemented coffin" as a "breathing Cadaver"... which is one of the reasons I am... still screaming.

There should be no misapprehension regarding my heart's intentions,

How could it be when my heart is so transparent... I am daring any One who may began to disparage me... to first walk in my shoes before They condemn me... and began start staring... stating that my state of Affairs are not... considerably sad...

The effective negation of my hopes have been driving me... considerably mad... and with every minute of existing that I've had...

Happiness has been in a state of atrophy...

I have long positioned that my entire existence has been comparable
To a walking abortion... I am a living, breathing... tragedy.

So after you hear these words and cringe... know that I too feel the
Same thing... since I'm unable to tame the pain that I've seen...

All throughout my life... so maybe this still explains... why the Caged
brothers still scream...

Because we're in prison.

21st Century Lynching

Convicted before birth... so no one really believes in my innocence... Deemed worthless from the outset, so they posit that I wasn't born Human anyway... and that my humanity can only come... in increments.

The black robe and the gavel has taken the place of the white robe And noose...

So as I prepare for my battles in the court room, being herded like Cattle... I've concluded that they don't care about the truth.

They want our youth to die... but to do so in slow motion occurring Through years... wasted... And my dried tears are continually being Tasted... And my brief notion of hope behind these walls of isolation has barely survived here...so I face it.

I'm being asphyxiated by the New Jim Crow's favorite statement, "Kaffir boy, here, take this life without parole"

But since they suppose that I wasn't born human, then they posit That I don't possess a soul.

This existence is choking me, my legs Kick, my arms flail, yet I move in slow Motion...

Perpetual pain preventing progress, meaning I fall into a mental Abyss of death... but it's like I'm screaming and yet choking...

But no words or sounds are being spoken.

Yet... wouldn't death imply life...

I feel the anguish is even worse at nights...so I subsist on nothing But pain... and no one cares that this system... is not right.

I'm being forced to deal with a prison term, yet I battle to expose The judicial system's intentions...

They placed a rope around my neck, so I choke, yet no one is willing To listen... to the alphabets dangling from my neck saying, Life Without Parole... this country's 21st Century Lynching Exhibition.

African Holocaust

I believe that I merely exist in the shadows of society... through My pending incarceration...

I would be remiss to not express that the judicial system is comparable to the gallows... in my eyes this land is a Bonafide heartless nation.

Society's general consensus is that my only intentions in life are

Surely to deceive... purely unworthy of a reprieve...

due to my heritage... as if I am not human... as if you prick me, my

Blood will not bleed...

Red.

As if you could asphyxiate me and I won't pass out because my lungs Also need to breathe...

And if this society continues to hate me then why do they believe

That I have no right to grieve.

This fact.

In bondage on a constant basis basing this on what I feel about Myself ... it's too much to deal with... without any help...

But I forge on because there is no other choice... there is nothing Else.

I sometimes wonder what life in America would look like if it was Defeated by German Nazis...

I'm conscious of their hate-filled yearnings of genocide, but it would be more easy to stomach because it wasn't filled with blatant Hypocrisy... hidden in a fictitious democracy.

Stating that our worthlessness is valid, so I can't view life through Rose colored lenses...

So the things that I have been forced to contend with...

Have left me broken... left me imprisoned... left me friendless.

So as I pretend that this isn't as horrible as I claim... I hold my Hands behind my back with my fingers crossed... since all seems lost... and I'm forced to deal with this 21st Century Lynching... called prison. Clearly this country's second African Holocaust

21 Years a Slave

I'm being haunted by memories... that vividly plays itself out...

Born hunted by an unforeseen enemy... a "cemented coffin"... trapped in prison... Trying to find a way out... is death the escape route?

They tell me... at least I'm not dead... but I don't only wish to survive... I have A notion... yes... I choose to live...

What I did was not what I was... but what I was... was merely a foolish kid...

I sought death... in an attempt to live.

This oddity comes in the strangest of thoughts... since it seems that only my Thoughts are all I have left...

It's not so much of an anomaly... that I ponder a day of being free... even if it

Means that I have to concede to the thoughts... of my own death.

In these 21 years as a slave... it has paved scenery so constant... but still

Excruciating...

It has me in truth hating this false reality & when I say I should be free

Since I am innocent they say... an innocent man... I am innocent, not... I

Am only imitating.

This causes the sun to no longer shine... the stars are black... the moon no longer glows... it

Slows... the concept of time... this is my cruelest foe...

Because he will not allow for my conscious to grow...

Plus I'm being sentenced to live... on death row.

To whom can I look forward to help me open the door to this cruel... cold... Sarcophagus...

I have long deposited into the heaven's that this anguish is unbearable... That the screams are stuck... inside of my esophagus.

So how shall I regain my freedom... when I never really cared for living...

The sad reality... that simply compounds this tragedy... is that I was already Enslaved... long before I was sent... to this wretched prison.

Invisible Man

I realize that I'm an invisible man... but I don't benefit... from not being
Seen...

My existence in horrible scenes...

Suffering first hand a first nature... & I'm more accustomed to it than I Am
with breathing... so I have no choice but to scream.

Internally...

The fact that I'm relegated as a "throw away"... constantly burns in me... So
my existence in prison is comparable to death... but yet I still yearn To be...
free...

So I fight prison.

It goes without say that injustice... is common place...

Our lives are drama laced & harsh penalties are applied eradicating guys
Like me from the streets... with the same complexion as the one on my Face.

Anguish I had to taste... so I brace the muscles in my stomach...

It was so prevalent in my existence... that it made no difference... if I Got
inside of a jet... & tried to run from it.

No escape.... standing before the masses... yet I'm really invisible... Society
doesn't wish to know the enigma called Marcos... because they are Quite
content... with deeming me an incorrigible, unredeemable... criminal. These
messages are subliminal... that's how they transmit...

My days seem like I'm buried inside of a congested bottomless pit.

With no oxygen to inhale... & this place breeds death on a epic mental
Scale...

Compounding it with my innocence... being alone & unseen inside of the
Wretched cell... & with each attempt at progress... I only seem to fail.

About the author

Marcos Gray is an ex-gang banger who has sought enlightenment and aggressively pursued education throughout his incarceration. He has obtained his G.E.D., completed half a dozen Northpark Theological Seminary classes, 3 DePaul University classes, 2 North-Western classes and a myriad of correspondence courses. This is the author's second published work.

Subconsciously Unconscious is available at Amazon.com and other internet book stores.